How to use
New
Testament
Greek
Study Aids

How to use *New Testament Greek Study Aids*

WALTER JERRY CLARK

LOIZEAUX BROTHERS
Neptune, New Jersey

FIRST EDITION, DECEMBER 1983

A publication of LOIZEAUX BROTHERS, Inc.

*A Nonprofit Organization Devoted to the Lord's Work
and to the Spread of His Truth*

Library of Congress Cataloging in Publication Data

Clark, Walter Jerry, 1952-
  How to use New Testament Greek study aids.

  Bibliography: pages 234-253
  1. Bible. N.T.—Study. 2. Greek language, Biblical.
  I. Title.
BS2530.C55 1983   487'.4'07   83-14889
ISBN 0-87213-079-7

PRINTED IN THE UNITED STATES OF AMERICA

*Dedicated
to my wife Anne,
who has so faithfully labored with me,
to my daughters Heather and Hannah
and to many other family members and friends
who have given help and encouragement,
but especially, of course,
to the One who is the central theme
not only of this book,
but of the Book of Books and of creation itself—
Our Lord and Saviour Jesus Christ*

CONTENTS

List of Abbreviations and Principal
Bible Versions Quoted

ASV: *American Standard Version* of 1901.

Amplified: *The Amplified Bible,* copyright the Lockman Foundation, published by Zondervan.

Berkeley: *The Holy Bible: The New Berkeley Version in Modern English,* copyright Zondervan.

Emphasized: *The Emphasized Bible,* by Joseph Rotherham, copyright Kregel Publications.

Expanded: *The New Testament: An Expanded Translation,* by Kenneth S. Wuest, copyright Wm. B. Eerdmans.

KJV: *King James Version.*

NASB: *New American Standard Bible,* copyright the Lockman Foundation.

NIV: *New International Version,* copyright the New York Bible Society International.

Phillips: *The New Testament in Modern English,* by J. B. Phillips, copyright Macmillan.

RSV: *Revised Standard Version,* copyright the National Council of the Churches of Christ in the U.S.A.

Williams: *The New Testament in the Language of the People,* by Charles Williams, copyright Edith S. Williams, published by Moody Press.

INTRODUCTION

A new fad is sweeping the land! William Barclay, the late Biblical expositor, is only one of many who have remarked on "the extraordinary interest in the Bible which exists today and which is becoming ever stronger. I do not think that there ever was a time when people were more interested in what the Bible has to say and what the Bible means" (*New Testament Words*).

To this remark we would reply, "Thank God!" and "No wonder!" We thank God for this interest because, even though to many people it may indeed be only a fad which will pass, we know from experience that for others what begins as curiosity may end as a life-changing experience. This is because "the word of God is quick [living] and powerful" (Hebrews 4:12 KJV).

And we say "no wonder" because the Bible is above all books eminently worthy of our interest and attention. It is a veritable mine of hidden treasures for those willing to take the time and effort to search them out (Proverbs 2:1-5; cf. Colossians 2:3).

This new interest in the Bible is not confined to modern versions, or indeed to *any* translations of the Word. Recent years have seen such an upsurge of interest in the original languages of the Bible, particularly New Testament Greek, that writers, editors, scholars, and publishers have combined to produce a large number of works solely for the benefit of those who wish to study the Greek Testament but who have no background in New Testament Greek.

Unfortunately, many Bible students still do not realize how easy and how rewarding it is for those with no previous knowledge of New Testament Greek to learn to use the Greek New Testament itself in their own studies. The purpose of this book is to introduce the wide field of Greek study aids and tools and to present such information as will enable them to be used most effectively. No language skills are necessary as a prerequisite; any such skills needed for particular tools will be acquired gradually and naturally as we consider these tools.

The wonderful world of the New Testament in the original Greek now lies open to any and all who wish to enter it—a world of riches and treasures beyond imagination. The question now is, Why wait? Let's begin to mine these hidden treasures of God's Word!

1

LIGHT FROM THE RUBBISH HEAPS

Imagine that you have opened your Bible to one of your favorite passages: the famous "love chapter" (1 Corinthians 13). However, instead of the familiar "Though I speak with the tongues of men and of angels" you are confronted with the following:

> Ἐὰν ταῖς γλώσσαις τῶν ἀνθρώπων λαλῶ
> καὶ τῶν ἀγγέλων, ἀγάπην δὲ μὴ ἔχω, γέγονα χαλκὸς
> ἠχῶν ἢ κύμβαλον ἀλαλάζον.

If you are like most of us, your reaction would probably be one of confusion and bewildered surprise. Perhaps you might even utter the well-worn cliché, "Well, it's Greek to me!"

And if you did, you'd be right!

Actually, if you had been a member of the church at Corinth, the original recipients of Paul's Corinthian Epistles sometime during the first century A.D., you would probably have been able to understand this passage with no trouble at all.

Most Christians realize that the New Testament was originally written in the Greek language, but, except for scholars and seminary students, our knowledge of New

Testament Greek rarely goes beyond the most superficial level. Most of us encounter Greek words occasionally in Bible commentaries, Sunday school literature, other Bible study publications, and even sermons. Usually, however, we just ignore these "interruptions" or wonder to ourselves, "Just what is Greek, anyway?"

What Is Greek?

Greek was originally and quite naturally the language of the people of Greece. Before about 330 B.C. the Greek language was confined for the most part to the Greeks alone. It was the language by which one Greek person communicated to another Greek person, and was rarely used by other nationalities. As in most countries of that day, there were many dialects or variations of the Greek tongue. The same is true in many Eastern countries today. For example, in India dozens of different dialects are spoken. Each region usually has its own dialect, and this dialect is often quite incomprehensible to the citizens of another region.

Four main dialects of the early Greek language were formerly identified. These were Attic, Ionic, Aeolic, and Doric. Each dialect derived its name from the specific region of the country in which it was spoken. Attic Greek became prominent around the fourth century B.C. because it was the tongue used by the great thinkers, philosophers, and politicians of Athens. Thus Attic, the language of the Greek classicists, became known as classical Greek.

For centuries after the Renaissance "rediscovery" of the great Greek writers, poets, and playwrights, Bible scholars recognized and puzzled over the differences between the Greek of the classical writers and the Greek of the New

Testament manuscripts. Giving the matter considerable thought, the scholars came to the conclusion that the Greek of the New Testament was a special language used only for religious writings. Some even went so far as to suggest that the Greek of the New Testament was actually a unique "holy" language which found its origin in the direct dictation of the Holy Spirit.

The Rubbish Heaps of Egypt

This opinion, like most arbitrary opinions based on insufficient evidence, was not to last forever, however. One day, around the turn of the last century, a young German pastor named Adolf Deissmann happened to be leafing through a section of a volume containing manuscripts from a collection of Greek papyri from Berlin. As he read, Deissmann was suddenly struck by the similarity of the language of these papyri to the language of the Greek New Testament.

"Papyrus" (plural "papyri," so-called because they were writings recorded on papyrus, a writing material made from the pith of a certain reed once common along the Nile) is a general name for the thousands of writings which have been discovered from the period around the birth of Christ, when Greek was an international language.

Various papyri have been brought to light as far back as 1752. Many of these were found in tombs or in earthen jars which had been discovered in the ruins of temples and houses. By far the greatest number, however, have been found in the rubbish heaps of Egypt.

These papyri were simply the everyday writings of the common people engaged in their ordinary, everyday affairs. They were not the literary works of that era but were the household papers, business records, personal letters, commercial notes and contracts, etc. These old papers were discarded and heaped on the outskirts of old Egyptian towns and villages, sometimes to a height of twenty to thirty feet. Probably out of a reverence for the written word (no matter how useless or banal), the citizens of these towns refused to burn their discarded papers, but instead simply threw them away.

These heaps of papyri were quickly covered by the sands of the shifting desert, and thus they remained almost perfectly preserved down through the ages to the present time. These papyri consist primarily of single sheets or fragments of sheets. Occasionally, however, whole baskets of official papers or documents have been discovered.

Deissmann, the young German pastor, recognized that the Greek of the New Testament, which was so dissimilar to the classical writings, was almost identical in language to these papyri. The New Testament, he boldly announced, was not written in a "holy language" at all, but in the common tongue of the common people!

As you could probably have anticipated, Deissmann's statement was greeted rather skeptically by his colleagues. However, time, research, and new discoveries have supported his conclusions. In recent decades, masses of new materials have been uncovered which confirm the view that most or all of the New Testament writings were, in their original form, written in the common rather than the learned form of the Greek language. About ten thousand of these early documents have been published, and this number is constantly growing, thus adding to our understanding of the New Testament.

This everyday form of the Greek tongue evident in the papyri came to be known as *koinē dialektos* ("the common speech"), now usually abbreviated as simply *koinē*.

Koinē Greek

What is *koinē?* Where did it originate? How does it differ from classical Greek? When Alexander the Great conquered the Medo-Persian Empire in his spread throughout the world, the knowledge of the Greek language spread also. The armies of Alexander remained in these conquered lands as armies of occupation. They soon settled among the conquered peoples, intermarried, built homes, and—in so doing—gradually imposed the Greek tongue on these people. Greek became a popularized language. Its grammatical and syntactical structure became simplified to serve the needs of the vast Grecian Empire. For centuries it served as the "lingua franca" of first the Greek Empire and then the conquering Roman Empire.

This language—known as Hellenistic Greek, from the word for the Greeks themselves, Hellenes—became the common tongue of the many diverse peoples of the vast region. Thus it became known as *koinē*, or common.

In the first century A.D., *koinē* was the language of the marketplace and the street corner. It was used for business, commerce, politics, and correspondence. In short, it was the everyday language of the common people going about their ordinary, day-to-day lives. *Koinē* Greek, therefore, compared with classical Greek is somewhat like the English we use today compared with the Elizabethan English of Shakespeare's time.

Obviously, this discovery that the New Testament was written originally in the language of ordinary people—rather than the language of the scholars—has given great impetus to the fast-growing movement of translating the Bible into everyday speech and idioms.

However, *koinē* Greek (like English today) was used in different ways by different people. Even within the confines of the New Testament itself, we can discern great differences of writing style and use. This results primarily from the different backgrounds of the various New Testament writers. John's writings, for example, which are so vivid, so poetic, so lofty in English, are in Greek quite simple and idiomatic, often containing expressions which reveal the Jewish background of the writer. John, who was born and raised in Judea, knew the Greek tongue but was not completely at home in it. He used the language correctly in his writings, but he did not write with the refinement, polish, and ease common to one who used Greek as his native tongue.

Paul, on the other hand, was educated well in the use of the Greek language, even though he also was a Hebrew by birth. Paul, therefore, wrote more forcefully and smoothly than John, but he still made use of some peculiarly Hebraic idioms which vividly reveal his origin.

Luke, who was by birth a Gentile and therefore born into the Greek *koinē* as his common speech, used the language at its best. His writings in the Greek are among the most masterful and literary in the entire Greek New Testament.

With all of this behind you, you may still be wondering, Why all the bother? I don't speak Greek; I speak English. After all, does it really matter what language the New Testament was written in? Is Greek *really* important to an understanding of the New Testament? Can't we just take a good English translation and leave the Greek to the scholars?

These are valid questions which deserve answers. But what are the answers? Let's find out.

2

GREEK, THE

UNTRANSLATABLE LANGUAGE

Why bother with New Testament Greek? Are there any *real* reasons why the average Bible student should concern himself with what has traditionally been considered a scholarly subject? The answer is an unequivocal yes.

Verbal Inspiration

The first and most important reason is because the words—not just the ideas, concepts, or thoughts—of Scripture are vitally important. "Each and every word of the Bible is a rare jewel, and each of them is set carefully in its own setting so as to reveal in its prisms the utmost glory of God. To pretend that any word that has proceeded from God is not worthy of our attention is to prove without question that such a one is a fool. . . . The responsibility of a Christian to know and to obey God's Word is a fearful one. It is awesome to think of the consequences of not knowing God's Word in all its variety, in all of its mysterious and august meaning. Without a diligent study, it is impossible to grow in grace and in the knowledge of the

Lord Jesus Christ" (The *New Englishman's Hebrew and Chaldee Concordance*).

Most evangelicals hold to the doctrine of the inspiration of the Bible. This doctrine is usually divided into two parts: the doctrine of plenary inspiration insists that *the whole Bible* is inspired; and the doctrine of verbal inspiration maintains that the Bible is inspired *in all its parts*—i.e., every individual word.

This doctrine of verbal inspiration is given different meanings and implications by different persons, but generally it is held to mean that God did not simply indicate the general ideas which He wished the Biblical writers to express, but that in His infinite wisdom and working through the Holy Spirit He inspired each writer to choose exactly the right word or phrase (out of his own vocabulary and usually out of his own experience) for the right place, purpose, and meaning.

In 1 Corinthians 2:9-16, one of the classic passages on the doctrine of verbal inspiration, Paul explains the fact that his words are not his own, but those of God: "Which things we also speak, not in words taught by human wisdom, but in those taught by the Spirit, combining spiritual thoughts with spiritual words" (1 Corinthians 2:13 NASB).

M.R. Vincent points out in *Word Studies in the New Testament* that the word rendered "combining" in this passage is *sunkrinō*, a word which appears only here and in 2 Corinthians 10:12, "where the meaning is clearly *compare.* . . . After speaking of spiritual *things* (vss. 11,12,13), Paul now speaks of the *forms* in which they are conveyed—spiritual *forms* or *words* answering to spiritual matters, and says we combine spiritual things with spiritual forms of expression. This would not be the case if we uttered the revelations of the Spirit in the speech of human wisdom."

Thus Paul claims not only that he was led by the Holy Spirit to express certain ideas but also that the forms or words which he used to express those ideas were inspired by the Holy Spirit.

Of course, this may not have been a conscious process; Paul may not have known that he was writing Scripture at the time he wrote it. The result, however, is the same in any case.

This doctrine of verbal inspiration explains why there are many differences in the style of the various Biblical writers, even though each was inspired by the same Holy Spirit. These differences resulted from their different backgrounds, vocabularies, and knowledge of the Greek language.

Since the Holy Spirit worked through those individuals whom He chose personally, the effect is that we have a Book perfectly inspired in all its parts, even down to the individual words.

What does this have to do with New Testament Greek? Simply this: it is obvious that, since the New Testament was originally written in Greek, the doctrine of verbal inspiration applies to the original language only, and not to any translation in any other language, whether ancient or modern.

How important, then, to be able to study the Bible in the light of the original languages!

The Changing English Language

There is another reason for making the original languages the basis of our studies: the English language (as well as all living languages) is in a state of constant change. Greek (that is, the Greek of the New Testament), on the other hand, no longer changes or fluctuates.

For example, if we had been living when the Authorized Version of the Bible (the King James Version) was first published, in 1611, we would probably have been able to understand most of what we read in pretty much the exact sense that the translators had intended it to be understood. To us, the writing would have seemed perfectly straightforward and direct—simple, ordinary writing.

However, few languages in history have changed as much as the English language has during the past few centuries. As a result, many words or phrases which were in common use in the sixteenth and seventeenth centuries have since either changed in meaning or become obsolete. The American Bible Society has compiled a comparatively brief list of archaic and obsolete words and phrases from the Authorized Version. This list runs to over six hundred items.

Translator Edgar J. Goodspeed remarked in the Preface to *The Complete Bible: An American Translation*:

> The English of King James's day is not wholly natural or clear to the average man at the present time. In common everyday speech "thou," "thee," and "thy" are no longer used. The use of "vinegar" in the sense of a wine or liquor for drinking has long since ceased to be recognized. "To ear" in the sense of "to plow" or "to till" is obsolete; so are "marish" for "marsh"; "scrabble" for "scratch" and many others. (Also) time has wrought changes in the usage of words. The translators of the King James Version were casting no aspersion upon the character of womankind in general when they said, "Who can find a virtuous woman?" But today, when applied to woman, the word will almost inevitably be taken in a more specialized sense, and so be misunderstood. The word "prevent" once meant "to anticipate," but is now used in the sense of "to hinder"; consequently its old usage in passages like Psalm 119:147f. puzzles modern readers. Facts like these make the reading of the Bible a scholarly rather than a religious exercise.

Jay Green has tested the "unintelligibility" of the King James Version on hundreds of persons and points out that not one person in fifty can translate Paul's statement in 2 Corinthians 8:1—"we do you to wit of the grace of God"—into their own native, everyday English, which is simply, "we make known to you the grace of God" (*The Interlinear Greek-English New Testament*).

There is another way in which the archaic language of the King James Version can be confusing. This is simply through word order. For example, in Matthew 4:1 we read, "Then was Jesus led up of the Spirit into the wilderness." While this is perfectly understandable, it is no longer the custom to split a compound verb in this manner. The New American Standard Bible renders it more modernly as, "Then Jesus was led up by the Spirit into the wilderness." Similarly, in Matthew 5:17 we have "Think not that I am come to destroy the law or the prophets" in the King James Version, but "Do not think that I came to abolish the Law or the Prophets" in the NASB.

But, you may ask, can't all of these problems be overcome by using a dependable modern-language version instead of bothering with New Testament Greek? To a certain extent they can. Many of the new translations are quite helpful. But here again there are problems.

As we have stated, English changes at an amazingly rapid pace. There have been approximately a hundred translations of the Bible made during the last hundred years. Many of these, such as the American Standard Version of 1901, are excellent and accurate versions, but are already becoming archaic to such an extent that they themselves are being revised and modernized. As long as the English language is used daily by millions of people, the language is in a constant state of change, and new versions will continually be required.

How then are we to evaluate these new versions that have appeared and that will appear? Obviously, by their accuracy and faithfulness to the original texts.

Wycliffe's version of the Bible, which first appeared about 1384, was translated from the Latin Vulgate, but ever since the time of Tyndale (his New Testament was first published in 1525), every major Protestant translation has been made from the original Hebrew and Greek texts. From the much-beloved King James Version to the most recent Good News Bible and New International Version, the basis has been the rock-bottom original languages. The importance of being familiar with the original wording on which these translations are based is obvious.

And there is another problem with English translations: the confusing number of them which are available. With over two dozen major translations available on the shelves of the average Christian bookstore at the present time, how is the Christian to know which version to choose?

Unfortunately, there is often controversy over the topic of Bible translations, a controversy which is stirred up by the appearance of each new version. Theodore Epp, writing in *Good News Broadcaster* (January 1977) notes that "the translation controversy has once more entered an almost belligerent stage." He points out, however, that "although the controversy over translations is an especially heated one at this time, it is not something new. Actually, controversy over translations became so serious in the Middle Ages that a few translators were imprisoned, and some were even persecuted to death."

In connection with the various Bible translations available, a certain knowledge of the original languages is necessary for several reasons.

1. The first reason is *discernment.* "Discernment" or

"distinguishing of spirits" is listed as one of the gifts of the Spirit (1 Corinthians 12:10) and is certainly one that is much needed today. Although most modern translations are dependable, there are a few which are not. These are produced and supported primarily by cults, cliques, and small special-interest groups. We need to be able to distinguish between those which are relatively faithful to the original text and those which deliberately distort it. For example, there are at least two versions available which render John 1:1 as: "In the beginning was the Word . . . and the Word was a god," or to that effect. In such cases, the groups or persons responsible do not believe in the full deity of Christ—a cardinal doctrine of the great majority of Christians for the past two thousand years—and therefore reflect their beliefs in their translations. The "proofs" offered for this rendering can appear impressive and even convincing to those unfamiliar with New Testament Greek. Without a working knowledge of the original language of the New Testament, how can we decide which rendering in any given case is actually the correct one?

2. Another reason for having some knowledge of New Testament Greek has to do with *avoiding confusion*. Even a casual glance at the many versions available will show some startling differences, even between the major reputable versions. In such translations, this is not done deliberately to pervert the Scriptures (as with the above example) but rather results from honest differences of opinion relating to the Greek text. Unless we realize and understand the reasons for these differences between different versions, we can become confused and discouraged in our Bible study, not knowing which version to use, or which one to trust.

3. A knowledge of the original will also help us to *avoid*

the various controversies over translations. Those people who defend particular versions and attack others usually have little or no knowledge of the original languages. Most such controversies are not generated by persons with genuinely evil or malicious intentions, however; they simply arise from ignorance and the quite common attitude of feeling threatened by anything new or different. This can be avoided by becoming aware of the reasons for the differences in versions. Knowledge produces tolerance of other people's beliefs and preferences, and a diffusion of knowledge regarding the Greek New Testament would go a long way toward stilling the stormy waters of controversy over translations.

4. A fourth reason for acquiring some ability in the use of Greek study aids relates to the effective use of translations. This will be discussed more fully a little later on.

The Untranslatable Language

However, there is an even more important reason for making the Greek New Testament the basis of our studies rather than any English version, no matter how well made. This is the fact that Greek is in some ways an untranslatable language.

"Translation is at best an echo," wrote George Borrow, and Cervantes concurred when he stated that reading a translation was "like viewing a piece of tapestry on the wrong side where, though the figures are distinguishable, yet there are so many ends and threads that the beauty and exactness of the work is obscured."

What is basically true of rendering from any language to any other language is especially true of the incredibly rich and varied Greek language.

William Barclay, the popular Bible expositor, remarks on this fact in his *New Testament Words*:

Translation from one language into another is in one sense impossible. It is always possible to translate words with accuracy when they refer to *things*. A chair is a chair in any language. But it is a different matter when it is a question of *ideas*. In that case some words need, not another to translate them, but a phrase, or a sentence, or even a paragraph. Further, words have associations. They have associations with people, with history, with ideas, with other words, and these associations give words a certain flavour which cannot be rendered in translation, but which affects the meaning and significance in the most important way.

Colwell and Tune stress the importance of studying New Testament Greek by arguing, "There is no such thing as *the* correct translation . . . for there is no single Greek word that has an *exact* equivalent in a single English word." They give, as an example, the meaning of one of the simplest Greek words, *kai,* which means basically "and." However, as they point out, "*kai* not only means 'and'; it also means 'also,' 'even,' 'and yet'; and in some instances (in Mark's usage, for example) it does not mean anything that can be rendered by a specific word in English. The rest of the sentence (plus the sentence before and after) tells what it means, and there may be several good translations" (*A Beginner's Reader-Grammar for New Testament Greek*).

A. T. Robertson, in his popular *Word Pictures in the New Testament,* agrees with this when he maintains that "it is impossible to translate all of one language into another. Much can be carried over, but not all. Delicate shades of meaning defy the translator."

When we say that Greek is untranslatable, we do not mean that it is totally impossible to explain the meaning of a Greek word or phrase in English words. Rather, we mean that it often requires so many words to adequately describe the meaning and connotations of a Greek word that we cannot do so in the ordinary translation which strives for a minimum of words with the maximum ease in readability. To *adequately* render some Greek words often requires so many words that we end up not with a strict translation but actually with a sort of translation plus commentary, or paraphrase, on the Greek text which is usually quite awkward for use as a standard English Bible.

1. New Testament Greek is particularly full of implied meanings and hidden "associations" (as Barclay terms them) which add to the meaning and which, quite probably, would have been easily and automatically understood by Christians in New Testament times but which often escape us today. As a result of this fullness of implicit and explicit meanings, a Greek word may require several or even several dozen English words to render it adequately. A. T. Robertson points out one reason for this: "Language was originally pictographic. . . . Words have never gotten wholly away from the picture stage. These old Greek words in the New Testament are rich with meaning. They speak to us out of the past with lively images to those who have eyes to see" (*Word Pictures in the New Testament*).

Take, for example, the word "force" in Matthew 5:41: "And whoever shall force you to go one mile, go with him two" (NASB). This word is the Greek *aggareuō*. Marvin Vincent remarks on this word in his *Word Studies in the New Testament*:

This word throws the whole injunction into a picture which is entirely lost to the English reader. A man is travelling, and about to pass a post-station, where horses and messengers are kept in order to forward royal missives as quickly as possible. An official rushes out, seizes him, and forces him to go back and carry a letter to the next station, perhaps to the great detriment of his business. The word is of Persian origin, and denotes the impressment into service, which officials were empowered to make of any available persons or beasts on the great lines of roads where the royal mails were carried by relays of riders.

Possibly the most famous example of this richness of the Greek language is found in the words for "love." Greek has four different words to describe different aspects of what we term "love." In contrast, modern English has only one word. (The old word "charity" no longer carries the meaning and connotations which it originally had and is therefore not really suitable as a synonym for "love.") Only two of these Greek words are found in the New Testament, but these two are often confused by English readers and are rarely distinguished by translators. In the New Testament, *phileō* generally refers to an affectionate, emotional type of love or relationship which exists between friends, acquaintances, and members of a family. *Agapaō* (the noun form is *agapē*) is the selfless, divine love illustrated and defined in such familiar passages as John 3:16 and 1 Corinthians 13.

2. Another difficulty in translating from Greek to English lies in the fact that it is not always possible to render a Greek word by the same English word in every passage where the Greek word occurs. The meaning of a word can be affected by context, and every major translation occasionally renders a Greek word differently in different contexts.

Similarly, different Greek words are often rendered by the same English word (as with "love" above), thus obscuring the fact that there is a real, though perhaps slight, difference in the Greek text.

For example, almost a dozen different Greek words are rendered by the English word "know" in the New Testament—not only in the King James Version, but also in more accurate modern versions, such as the American Standard Version of 1901, the New American Standard Bible, and the Revised Standard Version. In fact, many of these Greek synonyms are so close in meaning that it would be virtually impossible to find a different English word to represent each Greek word.

It is important to realize the distinction, however, in such passages as John 21:17: "Peter was grieved because He said to him the third time, 'Do you love me?' and he said to Him, 'Lord, You know all things; You know that I love You' " (NASB). Here the first "know" is *oida,* the second *ginōskō.* *Oida* is generally taken to refer to absolute or intuitive knowledge, while *ginōskō* refers to knowledge gained by experience. Wuest renders this phrase, "Lord, as for You, all things You know positively. You know from experience that I have a friendly feeling and affection for You" (*The New Testament: An Expanded Translation*).

3. Perhaps one of the greatest problems in translation lies in attempting to render Greek tenses into English equivalents. This is often difficult because there are Greek tenses (such as the aorist) which have no real counterpart in English grammar. In fact, Greek tenses are not really "tenses" at all in the commonly accepted usage of the word. They are based not only on the *time* but also the *quality* or *characteristics* of the action described by the verb.

The Greek perfect tense, for example, is concerned with an action which has been completed in time past but which has continuing (and sometimes permanent) results. The emphasis is on the *result* of the action rather than on the action itself. For example, in Matthew 4:4, "It is written," the verb is actually perfect in tense, and some versions therefore render it, "It has been written." The emphasis, however, is not on the fact that it was actually written down in the past but that it still remains written down. Wuest reproduces this double meaning by translating, "It has been written and is at present on record."

4. Still another point where most English versions are not able to reproduce the Greek exactly is in word order. Most translations attempt to perceive the basic meaning of the sentence or phrase in the original, then rephrase the entire thing in contemporary idiom. This is because the word order of other languages often sounds jarring to English ears.

In Galatians 2:20, for example, Paul writes, "I have been crucified with Christ" (NASB). In the original, however, the emphasis is placed quite differently: "With *Christ* I have been crucified." In his writing, as in his life, Paul was always careful to put the emphasis where it rightly belongs—on Jesus Christ, the Lord and Saviour, not on Paul, the servant.

Commentaries and Translations

Some have suggested that the use of good commentaries makes unnecessary the study of Greek itself. However, one of the strongest arguments for learning to use Greek study aids is to be able to use both commentaries and modern translations more effectively. Studying New Testament Greek—even at the seminary level—is not intended to enable the student to discard all commentaries. In fact, almost all of the great commentaries are based on the Greek text, rather than on any particular English version, and such commentaries, as we will see, comprise one group of Greek study aids. Even commentaries designed for lay-men or general readers often make use of many Greek words and terms and, without at least a small amount of knowledge of the nature of New Testament Greek, the Bible student will be unable to gain the greatest bene-fit from either these or more detailed commentaries or translations.

For example, Charles Williams's *New Testament In The Language Of The People* is intended for the man on the street. Consequently, this version is relatively simple and straight-forward. However, much of Williams's important work in distinguishing Greek tenses and fine shades of meaning is lost to most readers. For example, he renders John 7:44 as, "And some of them wanted to arrest Him, but no one ventured to lay a hand upon Him." The footnote to this verse indicates that "ventured to lay" is "ingressive aorist." But how many students with no knowledge of Greek would know that this term refers to an action contemplated from its initiation or beginning rather than simply as a com-pleted action? This explains why Williams renders this as "ventured to lay" instead of, for example, "no one laid hands on Him," as in the New American Standard Bible. The reason for this distinction, though spelled out in the footnote, is obviously lost to the student with no under-standing of New Testament Greek, even though this is a "layman's" translation.

Also, a basic knowledge of Greek study aids enables the student to *supplement* the information contained in com-mentaries, as well as check its accuracy on occasion. Have you ever had the experience of looking at every commen-tary you could find in an effort to discover the meaning of a puzzling Scripture passage, only to have the commentary discuss and explain every question except the one you had? Actually, no two persons ever come up with the exact same questions when confronted with a passage in the Bible, and obviously no commentary can anticipate and answer every question that will be asked.

By being able to make use of Greek study aids, however, we have a pipeline to all the most important scholarly work that has been done on *every* word and grammatical situation in the New Testament. Being able to use Greek study aids will not answer every question you will ever have, but such aids will be an immense help in regard to almost every puzzling Bible passage. More and more you will find yourself using the original text to answer your questions. Will you still use commentaries? Of course. And your Bible study will still be based on your favorite English version, to a large extent. But now you will be able to enrich your study by going to the original text on your own!

Insight

By far the greatest benefit in being able to use Greek study aids lies in the impetus that it will give to your devotional life and the increased insight that it offers into the New Testament. Some years ago a young Texas circuit rider was given the oversight of three rural Texas churches. At one of the churches, the chairman of the board of trustees—a tall, gaunt cattleman—greeted the circuit rider and said, "Pastor, we sure are glad to have you preach to us. We want to help with the work. Is there anything you can see which needs improvement?"

The pastor's gaze lingered on the single small light bulb which hung from the ceiling. "I think that a chandelier would be most helpful," was his modest suggestion.

Some weeks later he mentioned it again. "Well, pastor," drawled the chairman, "we hit a little snag on that request. In the first place, none of us could spell it, so we couldn't order it. Furthermore, nobody here can even play one. Besides that, we all decided that the first thing this church needs is more light."

Obviously these trustees needed more light on the subject of chandeliers! The point of using this story is simply to illustrate that Greek study aids can be the best "chandelier" of all in our study of the New Testament.

The greatest joy from studying Greek comes in the wonderful light that is shed on our Bible studies. For many of us, the Bible has become so familiar that we no longer read it as a fresh, living book. The letters of Paul, for example, do not have the same immediacy and urgency for us that they had for their original first-century recipients. Many words and phrases have become theological catchwords, used freely by Christians with little real thought as to their original meaning.

Dr. Eugene Nida, Bible translator and theoretician, gives an example of this fact:

Some words become encrusted with our own linguistic tradition and only by returning to the Greek and Hebrew can we re-capture the fundamental significance of the message of God's revelation. One group of such words comprises "saint," "holy," "sanctify," and "sanctification." With only an understanding of the connotations of these words in English we gather the impression that the Bible is talking about a kind of sanctimonious, do-nothing religion, a twiddling of the thumbs in some pious atmosphere, the innocuous mumbling of well-memorized prayers, or the uninspired repetition of standard clichés which gain one the reputation of being spiritually-minded even though the heart may be wholly occupied with things of this world. The Greek root *hag-* is not just a synonym for good. Its primary significance is "set apart, consecrated, dedicated to the exclusive service of God." The moral content (of the word) comes from the nature of God and from the life which His worshippers are expected to live because they are consecrated to Him. Our holiness must reflect His holiness or it is not true holiness, only self-imposed piety (*God's Word in Man's Language*).

Dr. Nida reinforces the necessity of being able to use Greek study aids when he states that "there are some words which cannot be explained by all the detailed comments of exhaustive dictionaries."

Another example can be found in the word "hope." How encouraging to find that the word *elpis* ("hope" in such passages as Titus 1:2—"the hope of eternal life, which God, who cannot lie, promised long ages ago"—NASB) refers not simply to a vague desire but to a confident expectation! The word "hope" originally meant "trust or reliance," and this is still given as a primary meaning in most English dictionaries. Today, however, we use the word "hope" in casual use to express little more than a wish or desire. We say, "I *hope* it's not going to rain today," indicating that we would rather it didn't, but not that we really expect it not to.

Our "hope" of eternal life is not just a desire (which every logically thinking human being must have) but a confident expectation or assurance which rightly belongs only to those who have placed their trust in the Lord Jesus Christ. Since God, who cannot lie, promised it to us, eternal life is as certain as any fact in the universe.

We have seen that Greek is, in its essence, almost an untranslatable language. God, working in His infinite wisdom, chose the Greek language to reveal the precious truths of the New Testament, the new covenant in Christ's blood (see Matthew 26:28). Possibly no other language in the world is better suited for this purpose. In addition to being the most important language of New Testament times and the language of commerce, philosophy, and science, Greek is also a beautiful and expressive language. Few other languages contain so many shades of meaning, so many implied connotations, so much vital information in a single word. Few other languages are so flexible, so sensitive, so truly suited for the task of attempting to express the almost inexpressible—and certainly inexhaustible—truths about the love, grace, mercy, joy, kindness, wisdom, and power of God, who "spoke long ago . . . in the prophets . . . [but] in these days has spoken to us in His Son" (Hebrews 1:1-2 NASB).

The World of Greek Study Aids

Yet, as Dr. Eugene Nida has admitted, "for the average layman, and for some theological students, Greek is regarded as 'quite impossible.' "

Fortunately, this does not need to be the case. Thanks to modern scholarship, the average Bible reader and student today can share in the wealth of the Greek New Testament without ever taking a single seminary course or even learning a single word of Greek! The remainder of this book will be concerned with accomplishing this goal. This book is not written for Greek students (though they may find some encouragement here), nor is it a course in New Testament Greek—a subject too involved to be covered fully in such a brief space. Rather, this work is written for those who do not have the time, opportunity, or even desire to learn New Testament Greek from the bottom to the top, yet would like to have the benefit of a knowledge of the original language of the New Testament.

The simple theme of this book is "How to use Greek study aids." This goal will be approached systematically, beginning with the simplest aids and moving on to the more difficult ones. In the next chapter we will get a bird's-eye view of the world of Greek study aids. What aids are available to the average reader? How can we learn to use them without learning Greek?

But first we need to remember one thing: learning to use Greek study aids can revolutionize and revitalize our Christian life, but not without our help! We will never get any more out of any Bible study than we put into it. The attitude with which we approach our study of the Bible and our consideration of God's Word is far more important than any study aids we might employ. A prayerful attitude, a sincere desire to learn, a conscious knowledge of God's reality and presence—these things will assure us of God's help as we attempt to understand the Bible. And with God helping us, how can we fail?

Finally, in any study of the Bible we need to remember the words of the seventeenth-century English clergyman Thomas Adams: "The Bible is to us what the star was to the wise men; but if we spend all our time in gazing upon it, observing its motions, admiring its splendor, without being led to Christ by it, the use of it will be lost to us."

Not only do we need to be led to Christ, but after we have become Christians we also need to be led into a closer, more consecrated walk with Christ, and into a more satisfying and meaningful Christian life.

3

BEGINNING THE JOURNEY

The Bible student of today is much more fortunate than he may realize. Great strides have been made in scientific learning and scholarship. Though we may look with dis-may at some of the results of our technological explosion (pollution, atomic bombs, energy depletion, etc.), yet there are advantages to be reaped as well. As Moses said to the children of Israel in his farewell speech, "I am setting before you today a blessing and a curse" (Deuteronomy 11:26-29 NASB). The curses of modern technology have been publicized a great deal, but what are some of the blessings, especially as regards the Bible student?

The science and art of printing have undergone numer-ous changes since the days when each Bible or book had to be copied by hand and cost a year's wages to purchase. We have come a long way from Gutenberg's revolutionary movable type to the giant printing presses of today with their new methods of lithography and other printing marvels.

Today most people, at least in the Western world, can own and buy books for only a small amount of money. This fact, coupled with new methods of restoring old man-uscripts, greatly improved transportation and communica-tion facilities, and literally millions of hours of study on the part of Bible scholars (not to mention the thousands of archaeological discoveries made in the last century which have shed new light on the Bible), have combined to place the Bible student of today in a most advantageous position. The knowledge and learning of the past thirty-five centuries of Biblical studies are now available to almost everyone. Knowledge of the Bible in the original languages is now the possession of "everyman"—not just the scholars.

There was a time when it was illegal for a Christian layman to own a Bible at all. It was once illegal to translate the Bible into the English language. The Bible was considered to be the private property of an elite class of scholars and ecclesiastical officials.

After this obstacle was met and overcome, however, a new problem arose. This problem was more subtle: it existed because of educational and psychological reasons rather than by legal mandate. For many years, laymen were expected neither to know nor even care about such matters as Hebrew and Greek. As a result, books written about such topics, as well as many commentaries, required a high degree of scholarly knowledge on the part of the reader. Most books dealing with the Bible from the standpoint of the original languages were therefore over the heads of the vast majority of Christians. As a result, the average layman of former days could truthfully say about most Bible expositions written by scholars, "It's Greek to me!"

Today, thanks to the achievements mentioned earlier, this is no longer so. Any layman with an interest in the Bible can, by making use of the many study aids available, discover for himself the riches and treasures of the Bible in the original languages.

But many laymen are still hesitant to approach a study

of the Bible's original languages; many get glassy-eyed at
the mere mention of Greek. This attitude, unfortunately,
results from not realizing how simple and truly enjoyable
such study can be. The purpose of this book is to help
break the ice and encourage the Bible student to form an
acquaintance with many different types of Greek study
aids.

This chapter will introduce the various types of Greek
aids that are available. These will be divided into several
categories. Every single such aid cannot, of course, be
considered in this book (though a relatively complete list
of such works in print will be found in Appendix C), but
some aids of each type, and *all* the major works, will be
considered in detail. This will provide enough information
to facilitate use of almost any Greek study aid.

Since new aids are continually being written and published, any such study as this one must of necessity grow
gradually obsolete. However, a great many of the works
considered are standard works in their fields and have
been around for decades (and will probably be around for
many more to come). Also, any new works released will
generally fit into the same basic categories considered here,
so that the reader familiar with these standard works will
be able to use any new ones which might appear.

Greek study aids can generally be reduced to two main
categories: (A) those intended exclusively or primarily for
English readers; and (B) those intended for Greek readers.
The difference, of course, is that those in the first category
do not necessitate or presume any knowledge of the Greek
language or alphabet or grammar on the part of the reader.
In many cases, the works in category A print Greek words
in English characters rather than Greek characters for the
convenience of English readers.

The works in category B usually assume at least some knowledge of New Testament Greek. The non-Greek reader can, however, learn to use these works with only a small amount of effort.

These two categories will be further subdivided into several other logical divisions. In this chapter we will simply glance at these divisions and consider some representative works as examples. In later chapters we will examine more works in detail and learn how to use them.

Study Aids for English Readers

1. *English and English-Greek Concordances.* Every Bible student is familiar with concordances. Any concordance is a great help in studying the Bible, but most are concerned with English words only. A number of concordances, however, are quite valuable for the student desiring knowledge of the original texts, and these comprise the most basic and simple Greek study aids.

Among the best-known of such works are *Strong's Exhaustive Concordance* and *Young's Analytical Concordance.* Both works are classics in their field and not only serve the necessary purpose of listing almost every word in the King James Bible but also provide a wealth of information about the original languages (not only Greek, but Hebrew as well), though each of these works has a different approach.

James Strong and Robert Young were both great Bible scholars of their day. Young, for example, is the author of the *Literal Translation of the Bible* and other works of a more scholarly nature. Both men, however, are remembered best for their concordances.

There is an essential difference between the two concordances:

Strong's Concordance lists every word in the Bible alpha-betically. Underneath each word is a list of all the places where this word occurs. At the end of each line of refer-ence is a small number which points you to one of two dictionaries contained in an appendix at the back of the book: a Hebrew-Chaldee dictionary for the Old Testament and a Greek dictionary for the New Testament. If one ignores the numbers, the work serves the same purpose as any other (less exhaustive) concordance (as, for example, *Cruden's* or *Clarke's* or the small one in the back of your Bible): that is, a listing of English words with the places in the Bible where that word occurs. By using these two dictionaries, however, one can determine where different words in the original are translated by the same word in English or where different words in English are renderings of the same word in the original. That is, simply by turning to the back of the book it is possible to determine the original word behind every English word in the Bible.

Young's Concordance, on the other hand, analyzes the words as they occur alphabetically. He lists the English words just as Strong does, but under each word the Bible references are subdivided according to the various words employed in the original. Young provides, also in appendices in the back of the book, lists of the various original words, along with the different ways in which they are translated and their frequency of occurrence.

Each work has its advantages. For example, *Strong's Con-cordance* provides more information about the original words, including derivations and more complete definitions than *Young's. Strong's* actually provides two complete, though brief, lexicons in addition to the concordance. *Young's Con-cordance,* on the other hand, is often more convenient for the busy student who doesn't wish to take the time to be turning frequently to the back of the book.

In addition to these two standard works, both based on the King James Version, enterprising publishers have also made available to the serious Bible student similarly arranged exhaustive and analytical concordances based on the New American Standard Bible; the Revised Standard Version; and the New International Version.

These two types of concordances, along with a number of others designed especially to provide information on the Greek New Testament, will be examined in more detail in Chapter Four.

2. *Translations and Study Bibles.* You may already own a number of Greek study aids without realizing it, but are you getting the maximum benefit from them? Several modern translations and a number of study or reference Bibles can be quite helpful to the English reader in determining fine shades of meaning in the Greek text.

One of the simplest ways in which modern translations can help is simply by illustrating the different ways in which any particular Greek word can be rendered. Obviously, the fuller the definition applied to any word, the clearer and more accurate our understanding of that word becomes. This is why *Merriam-Webster's Unabridged Dictionary* is, in a certain sense, more accurate than a pocket dictionary.

A parallel Bible or New Testament (of which there are a number available) is particularly helpful in such studies. Take, for example, the word *exartizō,* rendered "equipped" in 2 Timothy 3:17 NASB. By glancing at a number of other translations, we will find several different renderings which will help fill out and clarify the meaning of this Greek word. A few of the more familiar translations render this phrase as:

furnished completely unto every good work (ASV)
equipped for every good work (NASB)
thoroughly equipped for every good work (NIV)
well-fitted and thoroughly equipped for every good work
    (Amplified)
adequately equipped for all good work (Berkeley)
thoroughly equipped for every good enterprise (Williams)

Modern translations can also be helpful through their use of marginal notes and footnotes. Some versions abound with such reader aids. These notes often indicate different ways in which a particular Greek word or phrase can be rendered.

There are several modern translations available today which are intended expressly for the purpose of opening up the treasures of the Greek New Testament for the English reader. One is Kenneth Wuest's *Expanded Translation,* which has already been quoted in the last chapter. Dr. J. D. Pentecost, of Dallas Theological Seminary, remarked that "the student of the Scriptures who is without a personal knowledge of Greek will receive more help from Wuest's *Expanded Translation* than from any other translation available." This work, as the title indicates, does not attempt to render the Greek on a word-to-word basis, but adds as many words as are necessary to explain the meaning, connotations, and grammar of the original.

A similar class of aids comprises study or reference Bibles. Perhaps the best known such Bible among evangelicals is the Scofield (and New Scofield) Reference Bible, a work originally published in 1909 and later revised. The new edition appeared in 1967. This work has probably sold more copies than any other study Bible through the years and is still popular with many Christians.

While not everyone will agree with the interpretive notes

in this (or any other) study Bible, yet the English reader can gain a good deal of information about the Greek text by a careful use of such works.

Much of this information is provided in footnotes. For example, a footnote at Romans 6:11 indicates that the important word "reckon" (found a number of times in Romans in the King James Version) "does not mean *suppose* but *count on, rely upon,*" a conclusion which can be substantiated through the use of other study aids. This distinction is crucial to the interpretation of many passages where it occurs.

There are a number of other ways of using this and other study Bibles effectively, which will be examined in Chapter Five, along with a more detailed examination of a number of useful modern versions.

3. *English Word Studies and Commentaries.* When most people hear the phrase "Greek study aids for English readers," they probably think of various word study sets and volumes commonly seen on the shelves of Christian bookstores. One of the first works concerned exclusively with the New Testament from the standpoint of Greek words was Albert Bengel's *New Testament Word Studies* (originally published under the title *Gnomon* in 1742). This approach to the study of the New Testament proved quite popular and has been successfully imitated by a number of scholars over the years.

This type of work can actually be divided into two groups. The first group comprises works concerned with Greek words as individual words (in the same way that an English dictionary is concerned with English words) and not simply in relation to any one passage.

Perhaps the most familiar such work is W. E. Vine's *Expository Dictionary of New Testament Words.* As the title indicates, this work is essentially a dictionary. Every major word found in the English New Testament is listed in alphabetical order, and the various Greek words of which the English word is a rendering are discussed and analyzed.

As an example, Vine points out that the word *exartizō* (in the previous example) means "to fit out, to prepare perfectly, to complete for a special purpose . . . used of accomplishing days, Acts 21:5, i.e., of terminating a space of time; of being 'completely furnished,' by means of the Scriptures, for spiritual service, 2 Timothy 3:17."

Works in the second group in this category could actually be termed "commentaries." These works, like Bengel's *New Testament Word Studies,* consider the books of the New Testament verse by verse in the same manner as an ordinary commentary. The essential difference is that these works emphasize the important distinctions and insight to be found only in the Greek text.

A characteristic work in this group is Marvin R. Vincent's *Word Studies in the New Testament.* Vincent's work, unlike some others, presents Greek words in Greek rather than in transliterated English characters. The work, however, is not intended exclusively for Greek readers and is quite popular with laymen.

As Vincent remarks in the preface to his *Word Studies:* "Can the reader who knows no Greek be put in possession of these treasures (of the Greek New Testament)? Not of all; yet obviously of a goodly share of them." Vincent gives, as examples, some of the ways in which the English reader may be enriched through such study aids as his own.

1. Where a word has a history he may learn it.
2. He may form some acquaintance with Greek idioms.

3. He can be shown the picture or figure hidden away in a word.

4. He may learn something of Greek synonyms.

5. He may be shown how two English words, having apparently no connection with each other, are often expressed by the same Greek word.

6. He may be made to understand the reasons for many changes of rendering from an older version which, on their face, seem to him arbitrary and useless.

7. He can be taught something of the characteristic usage of words and phrases by different (New Testament) authors.

8. He can be shown the simpler distinctions between the Greek tenses and the force of the Greek article.

Such a description could well apply not only to the usage of Vincent's *Word Studies,* but to all Greek study aids as well.

Study Aids for Greek Readers

We now come to those aids intended *primarily* (though not necessarily exclusively) for Greek readers and students. Don't let this classification scare you, however. With only a small amount of effort and practice, such works can be used by the average Bible student.

1. *Lexicons and Greek-English Concordances.* The lexicon is one of the standard tools for the Bible expositor; indeed, it might be called *the* standard tool; certainly it is the one used most often. In view of this fact, the benefits to be derived from being able to use any Greek lexicon are immense.

A lexicon is simply a word-book. A Greek lexicon gives definitions of Greek words just as an English dictionary gives definitions of English words. In most cases, the words are listed alphabetically according to the Greek alphabet, with the definitions given in English. As an example, consider the definition given by Arndt and Gingrich's *Greek-English Lexicon* of the word *exartizō* (considered above). They define the word as "finish, complete; equip, furnish."

There are numerous lexicons available. These various lexicons could be divided into four main groups or types of works: (1) *the standard lexicon,* which simply lists the Greek words which appear in the New Testament along with their meanings (and related data) in the most impartial manner possible; (2) *the papyri lexicon,* which indicates the meanings of the words in the New Testament as used in common speech and everyday life in New Testament times (along with examples of such usage); (3) *the theological lexicon,* which attempts to define New Testament words not only from a philological but also from a theological standpoint (such works contain more interpretative material than the standard lexicons); (4) *the classical lexicon,* which is concerned not with New Testament words but with Greek words as used in classical Greek. Such works are intended primarily for the classical Greek scholar, not the New Testament scholar, but they can be valuable for purposes of comparison with New Testament words.

The greatest advantage of the standard lexicons mentioned above lies in their comprehensive and scholarly nature. Every word in the New Testament is considered from as objective a viewpoint as possible. Disadvantages of such works for the English reader include the fact that (except with a few lexicons which will be discussed later) you must know the Greek alphabet in order to find entries; and the fact that Greek is a highly inflected language. This simply means that both verbs and nouns change spelling according to tense, case, number, voice, mood, etc. Words

are listed in the lexicons according to their basic or dictionary form. Therefore one can rarely take a word as it appears in the Greek New Testament and find it *in that form*
in a standard lexicon.

For example, "I have written to you, fathers, because
you know Him who has been from the beginning" (1 John
2:14 NASB). Here the word which is rendered "I have
written" is *graphō* in Greek and would be found under that
form in a lexicon. In the actual passage, however, the word
appears as *egrapsa,* which is the proper form for *graphō* as
a first person, singular, aorist, active, indicative verb. However, if we were to try to find *egrapsa* in an ordinary lexicon, it would be a hopeless task, as we would not know
(without further information) that we were not even looking for the right first letter!

2. *Greek Word Studies and Commentaries.* This group of
study aids corresponds exactly to the word studies and
commentaries considered under Category A, with this exception: whereas *those* were intended primarily for the English reader, *these* are intended primarily for the Greek reader.

As in the former case, such works can be divided into
two groups. The first group deals with Greek words individually. One of the better-known works in this category
is *Synonyms in the New Testament,* by Richard C. Trench. This
classic volume was written by a man who was one of the
greatest scholars of his day and the Archbishop of the
Church of Ireland. It was first published in 1854. This work
considers several hundred words in the Greek New Testament and points out fine shades of meanings between
words which are often overlooked.

In the second group, we again have commentaries. One
of the more popular such works is *The Expositor's Greek
Testament,* edited by W. Robertson Nicoll. This work

contains the full text of the Greek Testament along with detailed expositions of the individual books by some of the greatest New Testament scholars of a former generation. Critical introductions and various related data are supplied, as with most commentaries, but the primary purpose of the book is to provide comments on the Greek text for the relatively advanced Greek reader.

The publisher's comment on Trench's *Synonyms* can also apply to this and similar works: "It is designed for the student who already has some working knowledge of the Greek language." This should not discourage the English reader, however, as the average Bible student can learn to use the various works in this section with only a minimum of effort by making use of simpler aids at the same time. In Chapter Eight we will look at these and other works and learn how to use them to gain the most effective benefits from them.

3. *Grammars and Grammatical Aids.* There is one type of Greek aid which we have deliberately omitted until now, for it is not exactly an aid: this is the Greek New Testament itself. All of the various aids we have mentioned can be used by the student without actually ever seeing a Greek New Testament itself! Can the non-Greek reader learn to use the Greek New Testament? Yes, and with less difficulties than might be thought possible.

In Chapters Four through Eight we are concerned with New Testament Greek. In Chapter Nine we will take a look at the Greek New Testament, see which ones are available, and look at some related subjects, including textual criticism. This introduction to the Greek Testament is preliminary to the study of Greek grammatical aids in Chapters Ten and Eleven. It is not necessary that the student own or even learn to use a Greek New Testament before studying these chapters. As with other aids, a great deal of information and insight can be garnered without ever using the Greek Testament itself. However, the ambitious reader may have a desire to work directly from the Greek text, especially with the proliferation of interlinear Greek Testaments in recent years, by the time he reaches the section on grammar. Therefore, we will consider the methods by which the English reader can work directly from the Greek Testament with a minimum of effort and knowledge.

Before considering the types of grammatical aids available, we need to caution against a wrong attitude toward Greek grammar. Far from being dull and dry, as many people might suppose, the study of Greek grammar can be fascinating. Bible expositors insist that there is as much, if not more, insight to be gained from a study of grammar as from considering New Testament words or vocabulary alone.

In fact, many of the most puzzling New Testament passages can be cleared up by a careful consideration of the grammar employed. For example, many of us have wondered about the passage in John 20:17 where the risen Lord says to Mary Magdalene, "Touch me not; for I am not yet ascended to my Father" (KJV). Many views have been advanced to explain this apparent contradiction with Matthew 28:9: "They came and held him by the feet" (KJV). Others have set forth ingenious theories as to *why* Jesus could not be touched before ascending to His Father. Actually, the words "touch me not" here are in a grammatical construction which forbids the *continuance* of an already ongoing action; in other words, "Stop clinging to me!" Mary was already holding Him at the time, but He insisted that she cease clinging to Him because He once again had to "be about His Father's business" (see Luke 2:49 KJV).

The works in this category can also be divided into two sections: grammars and grammatical aids. Those in the first category can again be considered from the standpoint of introductory grammars or courses for the beginning student and comprehensive standard grammars intended as reference works for the scholar.

The English reader, however, will get more benefit at first from grammatical aids than from standard grammars. One of the most useful works in this group is *An Analytical Greek Lexicon.* We have already mentioned one of the difficulties involved in the use of standard lexicons: the fact that such lexicons list words only in their basic or dictionary form, a form which rarely occurs in the New Testament (particularly in the case of verbs). It is, after all, the *changes* which take place in Greek words that give us the most information from a grammatical standpoint.

The *Analytical Greek Lexicon,* however, lists *every* word in the Greek Testament in the *exact* form in which it actually occurs. A grammatical analysis is given of each word along with the dictionary form of the word for locating the definition quickly in either this or any other standard lexicon.

The great convenience of such a work for the English reader is obvious. It is not necessary to learn the various forms of Greek words by memorization (a task which faces the seminary student) in order to discover what grammatical form a particular New Testament word has in any particular passage. It is only necessary to be able to locate the word in the lexicon—the method for which will be discussed in Chapters Ten and Eleven—and to understand some of the basic characteristics of Greek grammar.

Some miscellaneous Greek aids will also be considered—tapes, correspondence courses, etc.—along with some interesting ways in which your study aids can be put to use in regard to the Old Testament as well as the New Testament.

Finally, in the appendices will be discovered some useful information for pastors and teachers who wish to make more use of Greek in their work; some tables of Greek information conveniently arranged and presented for easy reference; and an annotated list of almost every Greek study aid in print.

Now let's get started on the first part of our journey into the wonderful world of New Testament Greek—a journey that could literally revolutionize our Christian lives!

4

ENGLISH AND

ENGLISH-GREEK CONCORDANCES

In this chapter we will examine the most basic group of Greek study aids—the concordances—and consider not only how to use them to derive the maximum benefits but also how to uncover some of the vast riches stored in the Greek New Testament waiting to be discovered by every Bible student.

The concordances we will be considering in this chapter can be divided into two basic types: English concordances and English-Greek concordances. The most representative example of the first type is *Strong's Exhaustive Concordance of the Bible*. The second type of works could also be termed analytical concordances; the most representative example of this group is *Young's Analytical Concordance to the Bible.*

There are two other concordances which fall into this second category: *The Layman's English-Greek Concordance,* by James Gall, and the *Critical Lexicon and Concordance to the English and Greek New Testament,* by E. W. Bullinger.

In this chapter we will be using primarily *Strong's* and *Young's* for our examples. One reason for this is that these two are the most readily available, being standard works in use for years. They are found in many libraries, even small ones, and most church libraries. Therefore the reader who wishes to experiment with the procedures laid down in this chapter will be able to easily obtain either or both of these two works. Another reason is that all such concordances currently available (in the category considered in this chapter) will fit one of these two groups: i.e., it will be either a *Strong's* type or a *Young's* type of concordance. Therefore the reader who can use these two works will be able instantly to use any other English or English-Greek concordance.

Strong's Versus Young's

Before considering how to use these two types of works, let's see what the real difference between these two concordances actually is.

As an example, let's take the word "furnished," which appears only four times in the New Testament (remember that all four of the works mentioned in this chapter are based on the King James Version), yet is a translation of *three different* Greek words.

Strong's Concordance lists this as follows:

furnished

M't 22:10 the wedding was *f.* with guests.	*4130*
M'r 14:15 large upper room *f.* and prepared.	*4766*
Lu 22:12 shew you a large upper room *f*:	*"*
2Ti 3:17 throughly *f.* unto all good works.	*1822*

The three different numbers tell us automatically that three different words are employed in the original. By turning to the Greek dictionary in the back of the concordance, we will be able to determine what these three words are.

Young's Concordance, on the other hand, gives the listing as follows:

FURNISH to—
To be filled, plēthomai
 Matt. 22:10 and the wedding was furnished with
To spread out, strōnnumi
 Mark 14:15 he will shew you a large upper room furnished
 Luke 22:12 he shall shew you a large upper room furnished
FURNISH thoroughly to—
To fit out, exartizō
 2 Ti. 3:17 throughly furnished unto all good works

We can see now why *Young's* is called an analytical concordance: because he analyzes the different words used in the Greek text and incorporates them into the listing itself.

The information provided leads to the same results in each case, and the reader must choose for himself which type of work is more to his preference in the long run. However, there are certain features of each work which makes one more useful in certain areas of New Testament study and the other more useful in other areas. We will therefore look at each concordance separately, first to determine how to use each work and then how to get the most benefit out of the peculiar features of each work.

Using Strong's Concordance

In regard to any of these concordances, there are a number of different ways in which they can be put to use. In general, we might categorize them as follows: (1) determining the Greek word which lies behind any particular English word in a New Testament passage; (2) comparing passages where the same Greek word is rendered by different English words (i.e., English synonyms); (3) comparing passages where different Greek words are rendered by the same English word (i.e., Greek synonyms); (4) comparing passages where related forms of a Greek word appear irrespective of the English rendering in order to form a fuller view of the Greek word; (5) determining word roots and derivations.

Almost any of the concordances considered in this chapter can be helpful in regard to these five areas of Bible study, but *Strong's Concordance* is particularly helpful when it comes to several of these.

First, let's consider the most basic use of *Strong's* special features. As the Abingdon edition of *Strong's* remarks: *Strong's* "enables the reader (lay person or scholar) to find the Hebrew, Chaldee, or Greek term which is the basis for translation of any significant word in the English Bible."

Books and Little Books

While *Strong's* is fairly simple to use, many people shy away from using it to its fullest extent. Many who own a copy of *Strong's* make use only of the English portion and totally neglect the special features. So prevalent has this practice become that some editions of *Strong's* have been released with the language aids deleted. By following the suggestions in this chapter, however, we will find that it is a simple matter to make use of these aids.

Let's take, as an example, the first word in the Greek New Testament: book. This occurs in Matthew 1:1: "The *book* of the generation of Jesus Christ." How do we go about determining just what word in the original Greek lies behind our English word "book"?

Step One. First, turn to the entries under "book" in the main section of *Strong's Concordance.* Notice that the entries in *Strong's* are arranged in exactly the same manner as in any other concordance: in alphabetical English order.

Under "book" you will notice a large number of listings of Old Testament passages. We will ignore these, since our interest is in Greek, the original language of the New Testament. The listing we are searching for—Matthew 1:1—is arranged as follows:

M't 1:1 the *b.* of the generation of Jesus   *976*

Notice carefully the number at the end of the listing, and note that it is in *italic* type. This is to distinguish it from the Old Testament listings, the numbers for which are in ordinary (Roman) type. The use of italic type refers us to the Greek dictionary located in the back of the concordance. In this case, the number is *976.*

Step Two. Turning to the Greek dictionary, it is a simple matter to locate *976.* Here the words are arranged in alphabetical Greek order rather than in English order, but the words are numbered consecutively so that we can virtually ignore the Greek characters at this stage of our study.

Now locating number *976,* we find the following entry:

976. βιβλος **biblos,** *bib'-los;* prop. the inner *burk* of the papyrus plant, i.e., (by impl.) a *sheet* or *scroll* of writing:—book.

Now let's analyze this a moment to discover exactly what information *Strong's* gives us. In each entry we find six different items: (1) the number of the Greek word; (2) the Greek word in the original Greek characters; (3) the Greek word transliterated into English characters; (4) the pronunciation of the Greek word; (5) the definition (along with derivations or root forms in many cases); (6) a complete list of the ways in which the Greek word is translated in the King James Version.

In this case (number *976*) the Greek word in Greek characters can be ignored by us for the moment. We note, however, that the word in English characters is *biblos*—a word which, as you might have guessed, forms the basis for our word "Bible." Thus the first word in the New Testament is actually "Bible," though it does not here have the connotations that we associate with it today.

The definition of the word shows us that when the New Testament refers to a "book," we are not to think of a bound volume such as our books today. Actually, a *biblos* is a roll or scroll, a sheet of papyrus (or sometimes other material) of various lengths which has been rolled up.

In each case, after the definition (the end of which is always indicated by a colon) *Strong's* lists *every* way in which the particular Greek word is rendered in the King James Version. In this case, *biblos* is rendered always by "book."

However, the converse is not always true: it is not necessarily the case that every time the word "book" appears in the New Testament, it is always the rendering of *biblos*. How can we find out whether this is the case? Let's return to the main part of the concordance, to the listings under the entry "book."

We can easily see that the word "book" appears a number of times in the New Testament. By glancing at the numbers at the end of each reference, we know that every time the number *976* appears, the Greek word is *biblos*. For example, see Mark 12:26, Luke 3:4, etc.

However, we note that two *other* numbers are also found here. Some references are followed by *975,* others by *974.* So even though we have discovered the Greek word behind "book" in Matthew 1:1, we can see that this Greek word is not the *only* Greek word rendered "book" in the King James Version. By examining these other words rendered "book," we pass from the category of simply determining what Greek word is the basis for a particular English word to the category of Greek synonyms.

Step One. Let's see what these other two words are. First we will take number *974,* which is found in Revelation 10:2,8,9,10 and nowhere else in this particular entry.

Step Two. Turning to the Greek dictionary in the back and locating number *974,* we find:

bibliaridion, a dimin. of 975; a *booklet*:—little book.

Dimin. refers to the diminutive form of a word, as will be seen from glancing at the list of abbreviations which precedes the Greek dictionary. Now, by turning to each of these four passages in the book of Revelation, we see that in each case *bibliaridion* is rendered by "little book." In this case, we have the derivation given: from *975.*

Step One. We see from the main concordance that 975 is found in a large number of passages. For example, it is used in Luke 4:17 ("And there was delivered to him the book of the prophet Esaias") and John 20:30 ("and many other signs truly did Jesus . . . which are not written in this book").

Number *975* is also found in Galatians 3:10, Hebrews 9:19 and 10:7, and a number of times in Revelation. (In fact, Revelation makes use of all three numbers: *974, 975,* and *976.*)

Step Two. Turning to the Greek dictionary, we find *975* listed as follows:

biblion, a dimin. of *976;* a *roll*:—bill, book, scroll, writing.

We have, therefore, three related words rendered "book" in the New Testament. The primary word is *biblos,* the word *biblion* is a diminutive of that, and *bibliaridion* is in turn a diminutive form of *biblion.* Now, by tracing each of these passages where the word "book" appears in our English versions and noting which of these three Greek words appears in each case, we can begin to see something of the incredible accuracy and attention to the smallest detail which characterizes the Greek New Testament. By a careful study of each passage along with context, we can see a slight, though certain, difference in meaning between these three words which tells us just why a certain word is used in a particular passage instead of one of the other words.

There is, however, a related study we could do to learn some more uses of *Strong's Concordance.* Note that of the three words, only *biblion* is rendered by words other than "book" in the New Testament. By looking at these passages, we will be moving into the category of English synonyms.

Step One. First, let's take the word "bill." Turning to the main section of the concordance, find the entry "bill." We note that the English word "bill" occurs only three times in the New Testament. In Mark 10:4 it is a rendering of number *975,* while in Luke 16:6-7 it is a rendering of number *1121.* This means that where "bill" appears in Mark 10:4 ("to write a bill of divorcement") we could substitute *biblion* or "roll," which *Strong's* gives as the primary meaning of *biblion:* "to write her a *biblion* (or 'roll') of divorcement."

Step Two. Number *975* is also rendered "scroll." Turning to the entry "scroll" in the main section of the concordance, we see that this word appears only once in the New

Testament: "And the heaven departed as a scroll when it is rolled together." Here, *975* appears after the reference, so we know that the word in the original is *biblion*: "the heaven departed as a *biblion* (or 'roll')."

Step Three. Number *975* is also rendered "writing." Turning now to the entry "writing," we find that this English word occurs four times in the New Testament. In Matthew 19:7 it translates *975*; in Luke 1:63, *4093*, and in John 19:19, *1125*. This tells us that the word *biblion* appears in Matthew 19:7: "to give a writing (*biblion* or 'roll') of divorcement."

Note, however, that there is something peculiar about one of these four references which needs to be explained. In Matthew 5:31 ("let him give her a writing of divorcement") you will note that no number at all appears in *Strong's* for this listing. Why is this? The reason is because there is *no* word in the Greek from which the specific word "writing" is rendered. The reason for this may be the fact that many times translators add words to complete a sentence grammatically or to make the meaning of a phrase more intelligible to the English reader; or the fact that, in some cases, a Greek word may be rendered by two or more English words. In this case, the phrase "writing of divorcement" is a rendering of only *one* Greek word.

When the reader encounters such a situation in *Strong's,* he should attempt to locate the Greek word under a related English word. In this case, for example, we could turn to the entry "divorcement" and we would see that number *647* is listed as rendering this phrase.

The Good News

We have examined *Strong's* in connection with its primary purpose of determining which Greek word is the basis for a particular English word, and we have also briefly considered the area of Greek and English synonyms. There is another advantage which *Strong's* has over other concordances, however, and this is in determining word roots and derivations and in revealing the pictures which lie hidden in many Greek words.

For our example, we will take the common word "gospel," a word used by us so often that we rarely think of its original significance.

Step One. First, we notice two listings in *Strong's Concordance*: one for "gospel" and another for the possessive, "gospel's." Secondly, we notice that the word does not appear in the Old Testament at all. Thirdly, we notice that all the listings are either *2097* or *2098,* with one exception: Galatians 3:8.

Step Two. Turning first to number *2097* in the dictionary in back, we find:

euaggelizō, from *2095* and *32*; to *announce good news* ("evangelize"), espec. the gospel:—declare, bring (declare, show) glad (good) tidings, preach (the gospel).

Step Three. Let's also look at number *2098* and compare it with *2097*:

euaggelion, from the same as *2097*; a *good message,* i.e. the gospel:—gospel.

We see then that both words are related: *2097* is the verb form and *2098* the noun form. We will find that this is commonly the case when there are two consecutive numbers in our listings.

Step Four. Now let's find the words from which these two words are derived. Both of them, you will notice, come from numbers *2095* and *32*. Looking at *2095*, we find that it is the word *eu,* which means basically "good." Number *32* is the common word *aggelos,* which means "messenger, one who bears a message." Thus the compound words refer either to "bringing good news" (*euaggelizō*) or to the "good news" which is brought (*euaggelion*).

Step Five. Now let's look at the single exception: in Galatians 3:8 ("the Scripture, foreseeing that God would justify the heathen through faith, preached before the gospel unto Abraham") the number is *4283.* The Greek dictionary tells us that this word is *proeuaggelizomai,* "to announce glad news in advance: preach before the gospel." We see then that this one word is the rendering of the entire phrase "preached before the gospel" in Galatians 3:8. We also notice that the word is derived from number *2097, euaggelizō.* The prefix *pro* ("before") is added to give the meaning "to announce before."

The meaning of "gospel" is obvious from this study: it is simply "good news." In fact, our English word "gospel" derives from the Old English word *godspel,* meaning "a good tale or good news."

Step Six. Now let's notice the variety of renderings under number *2097.* By tracing these listings, we can find the places where *euaggelizō* appears in the original, though we might not realize the connection with "gospel" (*euaggelion*) from using our English versions alone. We can also find out a little about what the gospel or good news really is. By finding the entry "tidings" in the main section of the concordance and seeing where the number *2097* appears, we find six passages (Luke 1:19; 2:10; 8:1; Acts 13:32; Romans 10:15; 1 Thessalonians 3:6) where *euaggelizō* is rendered variously "shew thee glad tidings," "bring you good tidings," "shewing the glad tidings," etc. One of the more well-known passages is Luke 2:10, where the message of the angels is "Fear not; for behold, I bring you good tidings of great joy, which shall be to all people." By examining these and other passages, we discover that the gospel of Jesus Christ really is good news in the broadest possible sense.

Step Seven. Let's look briefly at some of the other renderings of number *2097.* Under the listings for "declare," we find that this number is found in Acts 13:32, where "declare . . . glad tidings" is the translation of *euaggelizō.* Notice what this good news is: "How that the promise which was made to the fathers, God hath fulfilled the same unto us their children, in that He hath raised up Jesus again" (Acts 13:32-33).

Under the entry "declared," we find number *2097* in Revelation 10:7: "But in the days of the voice of the seventh angel, when he shall begin to sound, the mystery of God should be finished, as he hath declared to his servants the prophets." Or we might render it, "as he hath proclaimed the glad tidings or good news to his servants the prophets."

Step Eight. Now let's look under the entries "preach" and "preached." Number *2097* appears in a large number of passages, such as Luke 3:18: "And many other things in his exhortation preached [proclaimed good news] he unto the people." In several cases (such as Matthew 11:5; Luke 7:22; Acts 8:25; etc.), the phrase "preach or preached the gospel" is the rendering of this one word, *euaggelizō.*

From this study we can see that a "preacher" is essentially one who proclaims or announces the "good news." (There are, however, other words for "preach" in the New Testament which we will consider later.) There is really no need for Christians to go about with a perennial frown on their faces; we are essentially the bearers of good news and as such should be happy to be able to tell others of this good news about Jesus Christ, the Son of God and Saviour of the world. In this connection, it is also interesting to note that our word "evangelist"—a person whose primary purpose is to tell others about Jesus Christ—comes from these related words concerning the good news.

Hypocrisy and Hypocrites

We will take one more brief example to illustrate the advantages of *Strong's* in regard to word pictures, revealing hidden meanings of words which are often obscured through English technical terms. It is in this area of providing a great deal of information on word meanings and derivations that *Strong's* is far more helpful than the other concordances.

Step One. Let's take the words "hypocrisy" and "hypocrite," two very revealing words when we understand their Greek originals. First, we notice that there are two different numbers after the references under the entry "hypocrisy" in the main section of *Strong's Concordance.* James 3:17 is followed by *505*, while the other four listings are followed by *5272.*

Under "hypocrite" and "hypocrites" we notice a number of references, all followed by *5273*. We can already deduce from this that *5272* and *5273* are both forms of the same Greek word, though here, in contrast with the previous example, we do not have a noun and a verb, but two nouns.

Step Two. We will take the most-often used numbers first: *5272* and *5273*. Turning to the Greek dictionary, we find that these two numbers are listed as follows:

5272, **hupokrisis**; from 5271; *acting under* a feigned part, i.e. (fig.) *deceit* (*"hypocrisy"*):—condemnation, dissimulation, hypocrisy. 5273, **hupokritēs**; from 5271; an *actor under* an assumed character (*stage-player*), i.e. (fig.) a *dissembler* (*"hypocrite"*):—hypocrite.

We already see some interesting points: one of these is the obvious fact that our words "hypocrisy" and "hypocrite" are not *translations* but rather *transliterations* of Greek words. As with many other words in the New Testament (as, for example, "baptize," "baptism," "evangelize," and all proper names), the Greek words have come into our language in practically their original form. The meaning of the Greek word for "hypocrite" is a stage-player, one who pretends to be something that he isn't.

Step Three. Notice, however, that both of these words are derived from 5271. Let's look at the entry in *Strong's* Greek dictionary:

5271, **hypokrinomai**; mid. from 5279 and 2919; to *decide* (*speak* or *act*) under a false part, i.e. (fig.) *dissemble* (*pretend*):—feign.

Step Four. This word in turn refers us to two other words. When this happens, we can usually assume that we have a compound word—a word made up of two or more shorter words, one of which is usually a prefix.

Turning first to 5259, we find: "**hupo**; a primary preposition: *under*." Now turning to 2919, we find: "**krinō,** properly to *distinguish*, i.e. *decide* (mentally or judicially); by implication to *try, condemn, punish.*"

The word *hupokrinomai*, therefore, is formed from two words: *krinō,* the primary verb, meaning "to decide or distinguish," and *hupo,* a primary preposition used as a prefix, meaning basically "under." The meaning "to decide under" (which may sound unintelligible to us) came to be used as a special term for acting in stage plays, etc., where the characters performed their action *under the pretense* of being someone other than their real selves. A "hypocrite" was an actor who performed such stage roles.

When Jesus says, therefore, "Thou hypocrite, first cast out the beam out of thine own eye; and then shalt thou see clearly to cast out the mote out of thy brother's eye" (Matthew 7:5 KJV), He is referring to a person who judges someone else while *pretending* that he himself has no faults which need to be judged.

In Matthew 6:2,5,16 Jesus speaks of the "hypocritical" actions of those who pretend to be other than what they really are in regard to doing good works (such as giving money), praying, and fasting.

What a lesson for us today! Do we sometimes pretend to be more religious than we really are? Do we try to cultivate the image of being a humble servant of Christ, yet virtually ignore His demands on our time and possessions?

Many of us may see ourselves in the case of the woman whose pastor came to call. It was the custom of the pastor to read a chapter from the Bible and pray at the conclusion of his visit, so he asked for a Bible. The mother, with a great show of piety, said to her three-year-old daughter, "Darling, go and bring Mother the Book she loves best." The little girl dashed away. Soon she returned carrying the large catalog of a mail-order company!

Using Young's Concordance

Now let's turn to *Young's* for a consideration of the most representative example of the English-Greek or analytical type of concordance. What are some of the special features of such types of works?

As with *Strong's,* a primary purpose of *Young's* is also

simply to determine the Greek word which forms the basis for any particular English word. Young himself remarks in the preface to his concordance that his work enables the students "at a glance to find out Three Distinct Points— *First,* What is the *original* Hebrew or Greek of any ordinary word in his English Bible: *Second,* What is the *literal* and primitive meaning of every such original word: and *Third,* What are thoroughly true and reliable *parallel passages.*"

In some ways, however, *Young's* is actually more difficult to use in regard to the first point—determining the original Greek word of any particular English word—than *Strong's.*

As an example, if we were to try to find out what Greek word is the basis for "book" in Matthew 1:1 (as in a previous example) in *Young's* we would first find the entry "book." Then we would find the reference, Matthew 1:1, which is listed in *Young's* as:

Book, roll, biblos:
Matthew 1:1 The book of the generation of Jesus

However, we would also find a listing for "*A (little) book, roll, scroll, biblion*" and "*A little book, biblaridion*" (yes, it is spelled differently in *Young's* than in *Strong's*—we will discuss the reason for this in a later chapter). The convenience of *Young's* lies in the fact that one does not have to be constantly turning to the back of the book to find the Greek word employed. However, *Young's* can be confusing for the English reader at first glance because the references for a particular English word are not all arranged in Biblical order under the same heading (as in *Strong's*) but are separated into different groups according to the different words employed in the original.

Words for "World"

It can be somewhat difficult to find a particular reference in *Young's,* since we might have to search through a
number of different lists of references to find the reference
we want. However, this layout is ideal from the standpoint
of Greek synonyms, which is Young's "Third Point": determining "thoroughly true and reliable *parallel passages.*"
Whereas in *Strong's* we can recognize synonyms only by the
use of different numbers, and then we must turn to the
Greek dictionary to find the actual words employed, in
Young's the original words are conveniently displayed with
the proper references arranged underneath.

For example, let's take the word "world," a word badly
in need of clarification, as there are four different Greek
words all rendered by "world," not only in the King James
Version but in many modern versions as well.

Step One. Locating the entry "world" in *Young's,* we
find it separated into four different groups of references
according to the four different Greek words employed:
aiōn, gē, kosmos, and *oikoumenē.*

Step Two. The most common Greek word by far is *kosmos.*
Note that *Young's* gives the meaning of this word as "arrangement, beauty, world." The word (as we could discover by using more lexical aids) meant originally an "orderly
arrangement" or "adornment." It is from this latter meaning that we get the modern "cosmetic" and from the former
meaning our word "cosmos," representing the universe as
made up of an orderly arrangement of suns, moons, plan-
ets, galaxies, etc. Thus *kosmos* views the world not so much
as a planet or globe but as what we might term today the
"world order."

This word is used in such familiar passages as Matthew 5:14 ("ye are the light of the world") and Revelation 11:15 ("the kingdoms of this world are become the kingdoms of our Lord and of His Christ").

Step Three. The second-most-common word is *aiōn,* which Young defines as "age, indefinite time, dispensation." This word compares with our modern "aeon" or "eon," which Webster defines as an "age, a long, indefinite period of time."

Aiōn is found in many passages which speak of "the world (i.e., age) to come" (as, e.g., in Matthew 12:32; Mark 10:30; Luke 18:30; Ephesians 1:21; etc.) and all the passages which speak of "the end of the world" (e.g., Matthew 13:39,40,49; 24:3; 28:20). Actually, the often-heard phrase "end of the world" is never used in the New Testament; it is always the "end of the age."

Step Four. The third word is *oikoumenē,* the "habitable earth or land," as Young gives it. This word is found in a number of passages—for example, Acts 11:28: "And. . .Agabus. . .signified by the Spirit that there should be great dearth throughout all the world, which came to pass in the days of Claudius Caesar."

Step Five. The fourth word is *gē,* a word which is rendered "world" only once, in Revelation 13:3. The word means literally "land, earth," and the connection with our word "geology"—the science of the earth—is unmistakable.

With just this amount of information we can see a real and important difference between these four words. However, there is another feature of *Young's Concordance* which will give us a clearer view of these words and take us into the area of English synonyms at the same time. There are two appendices in the back of *Young's:* an index-lexicon to the Old Testament and similar work for the New Testament. In this study we will be concerned only with the second of these two aids. The index-lexicon to the New Testament lists the Greek words in the New Testament in alphabetical order according to the transliterated form of the Greek words (i.e., as spelled with English characters rather than Greek).

Step Six. Let's take the Greek word *kosmos.* Locating this word in the index-lexicon, we find:

KOSMOS κοσμοϛ

adorning	1
world	187

This information is similar to that found in the Greek dictionary of *Strong's*—i.e., he lists the Greek word (first in English, then in Greek characters) and then tabulates the various ways in which the word is rendered in the King James Version. However, he tells us something that Strong does not—how many times each rendering of the word is found. The importance of this lies in the fact that usually (though not always) the most-often-used rendering is the most characteristic and accurate definition of the Greek word in question.

Here we find that *kosmos* is rendered by "world" one hundred and eighty-seven times and by "adorning" once. Turning to the main section of the concordance, we find that "adorning" is found in 1 Peter 3:3, where Peter, speaking of Christian women, exhorts: "Whose adorning let it not be that outward adorning of plaiting the hair, and of wearing of gold, or of putting on of apparel." Notice that the second use of "adorning" is in italics in the King James Version, indicating that it was added by the translators to clarify the sense of the passage. Here "adorning" implies

the "orderly arrangement" of such beauty aids and measures as are mentioned in the passage.

Step Seven. Now let's locate the word *aiōn* in the index-
lexicon. Here we find that it is rendered "world" thirty-two
times, "age" twice, "beginning of the world" twice, "course"
once, "eternal" twice, "world began" once, and (in a compound phrase) "for ever" twenty-seven times. A form of
aiōn in combination with other words is the common expression for "for ever" in the New Testament. For example,
in Galatians 1:5 ("to whom be glory for ever and ever"),
the phrase is *eis tous aiōnas ton aiōnōn* (literally, "unto the
ages of the ages"). The word for "everlasting" in the New
Testament is also a form of *aiōn: aiōnios*. This word is found,
for example, in Matthew 18:8; 19:29; etc.

We see immediately that, whereas *kosmos* is "world" in
terms of the framework of man and his society (the world
order), *aiōn* refers to the "world" in its temporal sense. The
former word thus relates more to the way we normally use
the word "world" today in a wide variety of applications.

Step Eight. By glancing at *Young's* index-lexicon, we find
that *oikoumenē* is rendered "world" fourteen times and
"earth" once. The exception is found in Luke 21:26: "Things
which are coming on the earth"—i.e., the habitable world.

By looking at some of the other occurrences of
oikoumenē (which, incidentally, comes from a word signify-
ing "household"), we find that it clarifies some difficult
passages. For example, Luke 2:1 tells us about the decree
from Caesar Augustus that "all the world should be taxed."
Skeptics of the Bible laugh at such a statement, while others consider it merely a dramatic hyperbole. What a
difference it makes when we see that Luke was quite careful to use the word *oikoumenē* rather than *kosmos* or *gē* ! Thus
when he spoke of "all the world," he was referring to the

Roman Empire and its possessions, the civilized world at that time. Similarly, in Acts 17:6, where Paul is described as one of those who "have turned the world upside down," the word is *oikoumenē*.

Step Nine. *Gē* should now be traced in the index-lexicon. We see that the word is rendered "country" twice, "ground" eighteen times, "land" forty-two times, "world" once, and "earth" one hundred and eighty-eight times. The best meaning, then, is "earth," though (as with our English word "earth") *gē* may apply to land, dirt, ground, the countryside, or the globe as a whole.

Thus, even without using other lexical aids, we can see a clear distinction between these words, even though the rendering "world" is not entirely incorrect in any of the cases as we ourselves use "world" in a wide variety of meanings and applications. *Kosmos* is seen to apply to the world from the standpoint of "world order"; *aiōn* to the world in its temporal aspects, (i.e., duration); *oikoumenē* to the habitable or civilized world, the normal territory of trade and culture which to the people at the time of the Roman Empire represented the known world; and finally *gē,* which refers to the world in its purely physical aspects, either as land or as a globe.

Now, by checking our concordance and going through our Bible marking the places where each particular word appears, we should gain a great deal of insight not only into the meanings of these four words but into the Bible itself and why it uses each word as it does. Without a doubt the Bible is an amazingly accurate and exact book. There is no careless use of words such as we might do in our own writing or speaking, but an exact and incredibly accurate attention to details.

How and When Did God Speak?

There is often a relationship between words in Greek which is obscured even in the best English translations. In some cases, these words are cognates—as, for example, "saint," "sanctify," and "sanctification." In Greek these words are *hagios, hagiazō,* and *hagiasmos* respectively. The connection between these three words in Greek is obvious. And even though the English words are also cognates (all three derive from the Latin *sanctus,* "holy"), we often fail to realize this in our Bible reading and study.

Another example is found in 1 Corinthians 6:12: " 'Everything is permissible for me'—but I will not be mastered by anything" (NIV). Here the words "permissible" and "mastered" are both cognates in Greek, and anyone using the Greek New Testament would be able to see the relationship at a glance. "Permissible" is *exestin,* a word referring to what is "permitted, possible, proper." "Mastered" is *exousiazō,* which when used passively (as here) refers to being under someone's authority or power—i.e., requiring the permission of someone else in order to do something. It is practically impossible to show this close relationship in English without being awkward. We might render it as, "All things are permissible to me, but I will not get into any situation where I must obtain someone's permission to do things."

In other cases, two or more Greek words may have the same prefixes, giving an interesting connection not readily observed in English. To illustrate this, let's look at Hebrews 1:1-2, "God, who at sundry times and in divers manners spake in time past unto the fathers by the prophets, hath in these last days spoken unto us by His Son" (KJV).

In English "sundry" and "divers" are synonyms. Webster defines both as "various." But what is the actual
difference being implied in this passage? Why are two
different words used rather than the same word, as, for
example, "at various times and in various manners?" The
Revised Standard Version reads, "In many and various
ways God spoke of old to our fathers." What, if any, is the
distinction between "many and various" or "sundry and
divers," and what, if any, is the connection in Greek? To
answer these questions, let's turn to the main section of
Young's Concordance.

Step One. Consulting the listing for the word "sundry,"
we note first of all the interesting fact that this is the only
place in the entire Bible where the English word "sundry"
appears. We see also that Young lists the word not simply
as "sundry" but as "SUNDRY times, at —" showing that
all three words in English are the rendering of only one
Greek word. This word he gives as *polumerōs.*

Step Two. Young also gives a literal rendering of
polumerōs: "in many parts." We can see already that the
"times" of the King James Version refer not so much to
the different times that the revelation was made, but simply to the fact that it was made in different parts, segments,
or portions. That is, it was not made all at once, but
progressively, so that theologians speak of the "progressive revelation" of the Word of God.

Step Three. Locating *polumerōs* in the index-lexicon, we
discover another interesting fact: this is the only place in
the New Testament where the Greek word *polumerōs* appears. This means that there are no other passages for us
to compare in order to discover the rendering in other
contexts. However, we can find out more information about
this word, as we will discover shortly.

Step Four. Next, let's look at the word "divers" to see what the difference is between it and "sundry." Attempting to locate this word in the main section of *Young's,* we see an example of how such analytical concordances can be confusing to the English reader. Under the listing "divers," for example, we do not find Hebrews 1:1 listed, and a cursory glance might lead us to the conclusion that this verse is not even listed in *Young's.* However, by glancing down the column, we find that he lists not only "divers," but also:

DIVERS colours —
DIVERS manner, in —
DIVERS measures —
DIVERS places, in —
DIVERS seeds —
DIVERS weights —

These "multiword" listings show us that in each case one Greek (or Hebrew) word translates both or all three English words. Hebrews 1:1 is found under "DIVERS manners, in —." The word is given as *polutropōs,* and it is found (in this listing) only in Hebrews 1:1.

Step Five. We notice also that Young defines the word as meaning "in many ways or turns." Thus the complete phrase, according to Young, would read, "God, who in many parts and in many ways, spake in time past." Even without going any further with our studies, we have clarified this passage a great deal.

Step Six. Now by turning to the index-lexicon, we find another coincidence: the word *polutropōs* also appears only once in the New Testament, which is in this passage in Hebrews 1:1.

Step Seven. However, there is another interesting fact

concerning these two words: both words begin with the same prefix: *polu-merōs* and *polu-tropōs*. This indicates that the two words are related. By examining the index-lexicon again, we find this prefix: *polus*. *Polus* is rendered in a number of ways, the most common being "many" (one hundred and eighty-five times), "much" (seventy-one times) and "great" (fifty-nine times). Therefore the rendering "in many parts and in many ways" not only gives us the better meaning for *polus* but also shows the connection between the two words which is lost in many English versions.

Suppose, however, that we had traced these two words in *Strong's* rather than *Young's*—what would have been the result? We have already considered the method for locating words in *Strong's*, but we will review it briefly because it illustrates one feature of *Strong's* which may have confused some readers.

If we had traced the word "sundry" in *Strong's*, we would have found only one listing: Hebrews 1:1. Immediately following the listing is the number for the Greek word: *4181*. However, notice that (in some editions) there is an asterisk placed before the number. What does this mean? The asterisk, which is found in many places in *Strong's*, refers to the fact that this word has been changed in the English Revised Version of 1885 (ERV) and the American Standard Version of 1901 (ASV). A section in the back of these editions of *Strong's* indicates how this word has been rendered in these versions, the most popular "modern" versions in use at the time *Strong's* was first compiled. A dagger placed before a listing indicates that this word was changed only in the ERV; a double dagger refers to a change only in the ASV. Obviously, this information is of limited use to the modern reader and is consequently omitted in many editions of the concordance. However, for readers whose copies contain this information, these asterisks and daggers might be confusing without an explanation.

We will not take the time and space to trace these two Greek words step by step in Strong's, but, by turning to the Greek dictionary in the back (after having located both numbers by the usual method), we can compare the definitions which Strong gives and see exactly how these words relate to each other and in what way they are synonyms.

Polumerōs is defined as "various—as to time and agency"; *polutropōs* means "various—as to method or form." Therefore the phrase "in many parts and many ways" explains that God has spoken variously in times past; He has spoken through various agencies, through various men, and through various forms or methods. This "speaking" was not all done at one time, or as only one "speech" or address, but was delivered in different portions or segments at different times.

This revelation from God we have in the Bible and in His Son, Jesus Christ. The important thing to note is that God *does* speak to man, or, as Francis Schaeffer has noted, "He is there, and He is not silent." God still speaks today— through His Word, through His Holy Spirit, and through His servants. He speaks, but do we listen? More important, do we obey?

Word Pictures in Young's

We have considered the advantages of *Strong's Concordance* in regard to word roots, derivations, and word pictures. *Young's* also, though not as complete in the information he supplies, can be helpful in this area through the "primitive and literal" meanings which he offers for each Greek word. These literal meanings usually indicate, for example, the different parts of compound words, and it is these compound words which are so often full of meaning as word pictures.

For example, among some of the words rendered "covet" and "covetous" in the New Testament is *epithumeō* in Acts 20:33: "I have coveted no man's silver, or gold, or apparel." This word *epithumeō* means literally "to fix the mind on" anything. (It comes from *epi*, "upon," and *thumos*, "mind.") It refers, therefore, to having a "fixation" or "obsession" on anything (such as silver or gold) because of a desire to possess it. We have the same effect in our modern expressions "His mind was set on doing it," "His mind was made up," etc.

Another word is found in 1 Corinthians 14:39: "covet to prophesy." Here the word is *zēloō*, "to be zealous for," to go all out in pursuit of anything.

In 1 Timothy 6:10 ("the love of money is the root of all evil: which while some coveted after, they have erred from their faith") the word is *oregomai*, "to extend the arms for anything." This refers to a person who is always "reaching out" for money—his only thought is for "more, more, more."

In 1 Corinthians 5:10 ("fornicators . . . covetous . . . extortioners . . . idolators") the word is *pleonektēs*, "one who wishes more," one who is never satisfied with what he has, but always wants more.

In Luke 16:14 the Pharisees are described as "covetous." The word here is *philarguros*, "a lover of silver" (from *phileō*, "to have affection for, to love," and *arguros*, "silver"). The word, then, refers specifically to a "money-lover."

What a complete picture these five words give us of the often-mentioned sin of "coveting"! A covetous person is one who has his mind fixed on certain things, one who is zealous in his pursuit of these things, one who is always reaching out for them and is never satisfied with what he has, one who always wishes for more. Certain of these words could obviously be used in a good context (as in 1 Corinthians 14:39), but the fifth word illustrates what most of these words generally refer to: "love of silver," money, possessions. "Covetousness" in the bad sense can be applied to power, popularity, or *anything* which we do immoderately or to extremes and which is not sought from the standpoint of the highest spiritual good of ourselves and others.

Summary

We have gone into much more detail with the use of these concordances than we will do with most of the Greek study aids we will consider in later chapters. This is because these two works are for the English reader the most basic, the most usable, and the most comprehensive of any of the aids. In fact, some of the aids which we will consider later must be used in conjunction with concordances such as these. The importance of mastering their use is therefore obvious.

The procedures for these works, as we have seen, are quite simple. In *Strong's,* it is (1) locate the English word as given in the King James Version; (2) note the italicized number; (3) locate this number in the Greek dictionary in the back. Variations on this basic method include tracing the other renderings of this Greek word in the main section of the concordance; tracing the root and derivation of the Greek word; comparing the different Greek words which are translated by a single English word.

In *Young's,* we (1) locate the English word; (2) note the different analyzed entries and find our reference under the proper entry; (3) note the Greek word; (4) note the literal meaning. As with *Strong's,* variations include tracing the Greek word in the index-lexicon in the back; noting the various ways in which the Greek word is rendered and which renderings predominate; comparing the different Greek words found under a single English word.

Now try some words on your own to practice these procedures. For example, try finding the following.

1. The Greek word which forms the basis for a particular English word: joy (as in Galatians 5:22); mystery (as in Ephesians 1:9); justified (as in Romans 5:1).

2. Greek synonyms (different Greek words which render the same English word): master, servant, sickness, life, word, fool, wine.

3. English synonyms (different English words all rendered from the same Greek word): covenant/testament (*diathēkē*); bear witness/testify/bear record (*martureō*); grace/favor/pleasure (*charis*); Gentiles/nations/heathen (*ethnos*).

4. Word pictures (try tracing the roots and derivations of these words in *Strong's Concordance*): apostle, courteous, to teach (also consider under aspect of Greek synonyms).

5. Related Greek words: race/furlong; crucify/cross; eating/meat.

There are many more words to consider in these five categories; in fact, the possibilities are endless. Some of these words will be considered in the next few chapters.

5

TRANSLATIONS AND STUDY BIBLES

Many people would not consider the works in this chapter as Greek study aids, though they would certainly admit that they are valuable aids for study. Yet it is surprising how much insight the English reader can gain into the original language of the New Testament through such common and easily used works as translations and study Bibles.

In order to make the best use of such works, however, we need to consider the special features of these works and some simple and basic procedures for using them efficiently. But first we will look at the various types of aids available in this category.

Translations

It has often been maintained that (and this is good advice) every Bible student needs at least three translations. One of these should be a standard work suitable for church or Sunday school use, memorization, public reading, etc. There are many good versions available in this category, and most translations would probably be placed in this classification. Among the more popular are the King James Version, the American Standard Version of 1901, the

Revised Standard Version, the New American Standard Bible, the New International Version, the Modern English (New Berkeley) Version, and others.

Every Bible student should also have a study version. This term does not imply that standard versions are not suitable for study, because they certainly are, but that certain versions are intended almost exclusively for serious study purposes. These versions include the various literal and interlinear translations as well as certain specialized versions, which are rarely suitable for memorization, public reading, etc. Among the more well-known such works are Wuest's Expanded Translation, Young's Literal Translation, Marshall's Interlinear Version, the Amplified Bible, Rotherham's Emphasized Bible, etc.

A third group is the modern-language and paraphrase type of version. Again, these terms do not imply that they are necessarily less accurate than the others or that the other versions are not in modern language (many of them are), but that works are intended less for serious, detailed study than for devotional reading and for people with reading problems, new readers, young people, etc. This group also includes the paraphrase—a version which does not attempt word-for-word accuracy in regard to the Greek New Testament, but which is more concerned with discovering the meaning of the Greek phrase or sentence and then restating the entire phrase or sentence (or even paragraph) in modern language and idiom. Among the best-known works in this category are The Living Bible, Today's English Version (Good News Bible), and Phillip's New Testament in Modern English.

We will examine each category individually to discover different ways in which these versions can best be used by the English reader.

Standard Versions

The uses of standard versions in regard to Greek words are several.

1. The primary use is simply in comparing various renderings of words. Obviously, the more versions available for such a purpose, the wider variety of information which can be obtained. As we have stated, parallel versions are especially helpful for purposes of comparison, since they contain a number of translations conveniently arranged side by side. A number of such parallel versions are available, including: the Layman's Parallel New Testament, (Zondervan), which contains the Revised Standard Version, The Living New Testament, the Amplified New Testament, and the King James Version; and the Parallel Four-Translation New Testament (Back to the Bible Broadcast), containing the KJV, the NASB, the NIV, and the Amplified NT. The Eight-Translation New Testament (Tyndale) contains eight different modern versions.

An especially interesting work for purposes of comparison is the New Testament from Twenty-Six Translations (Zondervan). This work contains the complete text of the KJV plus "the most significant and clarifying variations from twenty-five later translations."

As an example of word comparison, let's take John 1:12: "But as many as received Him, to them gave He power to become the sons of God" (KJV). Comparing the word "sons" with other standard versions, we find the rendering "children" in ASV, RSV, NASB, and NIV.

Even without checking the original, we could assume that the Greek word here must mean "children" and not "sons." And this is the case. By checking *Strong's* or *Young's* concordances, we would find that the word here is *teknon* (plural *tekna*), a word which refers not simply to a male child (which is *huios*) but to "born ones," those born into a family without reference to sex.

Such translation studies are not conclusive, but by comparing a number of modern standard versions we can often arrive at the best definition or definitions of any particular word.

Take, for example, the "at sundry times and in divers manners" (Hebrews 1:1, see example in last chapter) of the KJV and compare it with the following renderings:

by divers portions and in divers manners (ASV)
in many portions and in many ways (NASB)
at many times and in various ways (NIV)
at various times and in many ways (New Berkeley)

2. A second way in which standard translations help is with the marginal notes or footnotes which they supply. Many people do not realize that the King James Version and other old versions contained marginal notes giving various alternative renderings of Greek words and phrases. Some editions of the KJV still retain these original marginal readings of the 1611 edition, but many do not, or else they substitute other marginal notes in their place.

For example, in Hebrews 12:2 ("looking unto Jesus, the author and finisher of our faith"), the original marginal note indicates that "author" is literally "beginner." That this reading is the more literal one can be easily confirmed by checking *Strong's Concordance.*

In many cases, the marginal readings of older versions found their way into the King James Version. For example, the Geneva Bible (of 1560) renders Acts 19:24, "For a certain man named Demetrius, a silversmith which made silver temples of Diana." The marginal reading, however, is "shrines" instead of "temples," a reading later adopted by the KJV translators. Similarly, some of the marginal renderings of the King James Version have found acceptance by later revisers (ASV, RSV, etc.) in lieu of the readings found in the text.

Some standard versions contain relatively few marginal notes and footnotes, while others are quite liberal in supplying such notes. One version that is particularly generous with footnotes is the New Berkeley Version in Modern English. For example, in the footnote to 1 Timothy 3:8 regarding deacons, the following information is given.

"Deacon" is translated from the Greek *diakonos,* meaning *servant, helper* and in later years *deacon,* as referring to a church officer. The seven men who were chosen to help the apostles by being of service to believers in Jerusalem, Acts 6:1-6, were the first appointed deacons. The noun "ministration," Acts 6:1, is *diakonia,* and the verb "serve," vs. 2, is *diakonein.*

By paying careful attention to such footnotes, and following up the references given, the reader can gain insight into Greek words, synonyms, related words, and much other information. In this way the "grand old Book" can become an exciting *new* book, and Bible study can become a pleasure rather than a duty or an obligation.

3. A third use of standard versions is in regard to Greek and English synonyms. Such versions are much more consistent in their treatment of Greek words and English equivalents than paraphrases and common-language versions, and the more-recent standard versions (such as the NASB) are generally much more consistent and dependable in this regard than the older versions (such as the KJV).

For example, the Greek word *krisis* (compare English "crisis") or "judgment" is rendered by three different words in John 5 in the King James Version: "judgment" in verse 22; "condemnation" in verse 24; and "damnation" in verse 29. In contrast, the New American Standard Bible renders *krisis* uniformly as "judgment" in all three passages, thus immensely clarifying the discourse in this chapter and preserving the connection between the three passages, which is obscured in the older version.

Study Versions

As helpful as standard versions are, the reader interested in gaining insight into the original Greek will probably gain more help from the various study versions.

Such versions can, of course, be used exactly in the same way as above. Some versions, however, are more useful in regard to the peculiar features of both Greek words and grammar. In this chapter, we will consider some versions from the standpoint of words or vocabulary; in later chapters we will look at them again, this time from a standpoint of grammar.

1. In regard to the various ways in which a Greek word can be rendered, the Amplified Bible is quite helpful. The introduction remarks, "The *Amplified New Testament* is designed to overcome much of this existing deficiency [of standard versions] by furnishing in one volume, and as the Greek text legitimately permits, multiple expressions for a richer, fuller, and more revealing appreciation of the divine message." As an example, it uses the verse, "Believe on the Lord Jesus Christ and thou shalt be saved" (Acts 16:31). As the Amplified Bible remarks:

What does the word "believe" mean? It is extremely important, for multitudes are pinning their hope of heaven upon it. Yet that word long ago ceased to convey, if it ever did, the sense of the original. The Greek word is *pisteuō* and means, "To adhere to, to cleave to; to trust, to have faith in; to rely on." [It] means an absolute personal reliance upon the Lord Jesus Christ as Saviour.

Thus this version renders Acts 16:31 by *amplifying* the word "believe":

Believe in and on the Lord Jesus Christ—that is, give yourself up to Him, take yourself out of your own keeping and entrust yourself into His keeping, and you will be saved.

Of course, in many situations not all of the word mean- ings given will be equally valid, and the student himself must decide which meaning is to be preferred in a particu- lar context.

2. A work especially helpful in regard to word pictures is Wuest's Expanded Translation. Word pictures refer to those Greek words which are so full of meaning that they require a whole phrase, sentence, or even paragraph to render them adequately.

For example, look at 2 Timothy 4:7 in a standard ver- sion:

I have fought the good fight, I have finished the course, I have kept the faith (NASB).

Now read this verse in Wuest's Expanded Translation:

The desperate, straining, agonizing contest marked by its beauty of technique, I like a wrestler have fought to the finish, and at present am resting in its victory. My race, I like a runner have finished, and at present am resting at the goal. The Faith com- mitted to my care, I like a soldier have kept safely through everlasting vigilance, and have delivered it again to my Captain.

Wuest brings out the fact that the words employed in these three phrases had specialized uses in the first century, referring to the Greek athletic games and to army life. Such distinctions give us much more insight into Paul's comparisons, but can hardly be brought out in a standard translation.

3. Word order in the original Greek cannot be brought out in a concordance, but can usually be determined through the use of literal translations. As we have remarked, the importance of word order lies in determining the emphasis as it is placed in the original.

Young's Literal Translation (by the author of the concordance) is usually quite dependable and consistent in reproducing as far as possible the word order of the Greek Testament. For example, Young renders 1 Peter 1:22:

> Your souls having purified in the obedience of the truth through the Spirit to brotherly love unfeigned, out of a pure heart one another love ye earnestly.

This word order is faithful to the original, but (as is often the case) sounds awkward to English ears.

Also in this class are the various interlinear versions. An interlinear is an edition which includes the text of the Greek New Testament with a literal, word-for-word translation between the lines of the Greek text. For example, 2 Timothy 4:7 in an interlinear would read:

τὸν	καλὸν	ἀγῶνα	ἠγώνισμαι,	τὸν	δρὸμον
the	good	fight	I-have-fought,	the	course
τετέλεκα,	τὴν	πίστιν	τετήρηκα·		
I-have-finished,	the	faith	I-have-kept		

The value of such versions is obvious, and we will learn to make a great deal of use of them. There are problems associated with using the Greek text directly, however, which make it difficult without the use of other aids. In Chapter Nine (and the following chapters), we will learn how to work directly from the Greek text and overcome the difficulties of word inflections, etc.

The English reader can at this point, however, make use of the interlinear English translation in exactly the same manner as any other literal translation. By glancing at the line of Greek text it is an easy matter to see where one Greek word is represented by a number of English words, and vice versa. Determining word order is also simple with such versions.

There are a number of interlinears available, including Marshall's and Berry's (both of these are available in different editions and from different publishers; a complete list of such works will be found in Appendix C).

Rotherham's Emphasized Bible could also be included in this group, since the renderings are quite literal and often reproduce the order of the Greek text. By the use of numerous types of symbols, Rotherham attempts to point out varying degrees of emphasis in the original. While the multiplicity of symbols used may be confusing at first, with careful study the value of this work will be appreciated more and more.

There is, however, one danger in regard to these and all "literal" versions. As is apparent from the differences between the various literal versions available, there are often conflicting ideas about what actually constitutes literalness. In fact, no literal translation is ever one hundred percent consistent in regard to rendering Greek words or grammar, and no two such translations ever coincide in all points. This simply illustrates the need to be able to make use of a number of Greek study aids in order to supplement such translations. It also graphically points out that *no* translation can ever hope to reproduce completely *all* the shades of meaning found in the Greek New Testament. As Kenneth Wuest points out: "In a translation which keeps to a minimum of words, that is, where one English word for instance is the translation of one Greek word, it is impossible for the translator to bring out all the shades of meaning in the Greek word" (*Untranslatable Riches from the Greek New Testament*).

Modern-Language Versions and Paraphrases

The primary use of works in this category lies in the area of comparison. Unlike the works in the above group, these translations do not attempt a word-for-word rendering, nor do they claim definitiveness for themselves. Quite often, however, a looser translation or paraphrase can bring out the peculiar coloring of the original in a way that standard works cannot.

For example, many of us have stumbled over the Biblical usage of the word "perfect." To us today, "perfect" usually means completely and totally without flaw, having reached a point where no further improvement is possible. When Paul says, in Philippians 3:15, "Let us, therefore, as many as be perfect, be thus minded" (KJV), we may question how we could ever be perfect in this life. And when we see that only a few verses earlier—in 3:12—Paul remarks, "Not as though I had already attained, either was already perfect," we may be ready to give up in despair and confusion.

To gain a better understanding of this word, let's note how some modern-language versions render this phrase. We include a standard version for comparison.

Let us therefore, as many as are perfect, have this attitude" (NASB).

All of us who are spiritually adult should think like this (Phillips, The New Testament in Modern English).

I hope all of you who are mature Christians will see eye-to-eye with me on these things (The Living Bible).

This must be how all of us who are mature Christians feel about life (The New Testament: A New Translation, by William Barclay).

Let us all, then, who are ripe in understanding, be thus minded (W. J. Conybeare, *The Epistles of Paul*).

The meaning of "perfect" is seen to be "mature" or "adult" in spiritual matters, not flawless perfection in our modern sense of the word (that is, one who never makes a single mistake).

Among the more valuable in this category are the paraphrases. Many people today have the idea that paraphrasing is a modern innovation. Actually, the history of paraphrasing the Bible can be traced to the Targums, paraphrases of the Hebrew Bible produced in the popular Aramaic tongue at the time of Jesus. These paraphrases originated in the explanatory remarks of Jewish rabbis in the synagogue services.

Paraphrasing the New Testament in English has been popular for hundreds of years. A recently rereleased such work is James Macknight's *Literal Translation of the Apostolical Epistles with Commentary* (i.e., paraphrase). This work was first published in 1795. The form of the work basically is a literal translation in one column with a paraphrase in a parallel column.

For example, James 5:2 carries a warning to rich men which reads in Macknight's literal translation, "Your riches are putrefied, and your garments are moth-eaten."

In the parallel paraphrase, this translation is indicated by italics, while the interpretative remarks are in ordinary type: *"Your riches,* your corn, wine and oil, which ye have amassed by injustice and rapine, *are putrefied, and your garments* in your wardrobes *are moth-eaten."*

Obviously, many of these paraphrased remarks are purely interpretative and are based on the opinion of the translator. In other cases, however, these added remarks are intended to clarify difficult Greek words or phrases and represent the conclusions of a scholar who has diligently studied the Greek text.

A good example of the later type of paraphrase is found in Sanday and Headlam's paraphrase of Romans 12:2: "Do not adopt *the external and fleeting fashion* of this world, but be ye transformed *in your inmost nature"* (*Romans*). Here the paraphrased remarks help to bring out the delicate shades of meaning found in the Greek words for "conformed" and "transformed" respectively (KJV).

Among the more recent paraphrases and common-language versions, those produced by Greek scholars are generally the most helpful. We have already seen an example from Charles Williams's New Testament in the Language of the People, a valuable work for any Bible student, but one which becomes even more valuable with a little knowledge of New Testament Greek.

Many of these versions are available in the parallel volumes already alluded to in previous examples. Since their usage corresponds to that of the standard versions, we will not multiply examples. A large list of such works, with comments, can be found in Appendix C.

Study Bibles

Almost every serious Bible student owns one or more study Bibles. A study Bible is simply an edition of a standard version (such as the KJV, RSV, or NASB) with study aids and notes added. Yet many of us do not make full use of the information on the original languages supplied by such works.

The amount of information furnished varies from work to work. Some editions are only slightly concerned with New Testament Greek, while others seem to concentrate on this subject. The information is usually provided in two ways: brief marginal notes and more comprehensive footnotes.

The New Scofield Reference Bible is typical in its presentation of this information. This work is based on the King James Version but incorporates significant word changes into the text. In other cases a more literal rendering is given in the margin. For example, Romans 6:11 reads, "Likewise reckon ye also yourselves to be dead indeed unto sin." The note at "likewise" remarks, "Literally, *even so.*" By tracing "likewise" in one of the concordances mentioned in the last chapter, we could verify this note. The word here is *houtōs,* a particle of affirmation, not one of logical comparison.

The footnotes often give Greek word studies—sometimes brief, at other times more complete. For example, the note to Romans 8:16 ("the Spirit Himself beareth witness with our spirit, that we are the children of God") points out that " 'Children' is from the Gk. *teknon* meaning *one born, a child,* and so in vv. 17,21; not, as in v. 14, 'sons' (Gk. *huios).*"

Two other reference Bibles with somewhat different approaches are The Companion Bible (Zondervan) and the Newberry Reference Bible (Kregel). The first work supplies an incredible amount of information on Greek words and synonyms. Much of this is supplied in marginal notes, but a great deal of it is found in the one hundred ninety-eight appendices in the back of the book.

Suppose, for example, we were studying Matthew 4:8-10—the temptation of Christ involving the worship of Satan. The note at the first occurence of "worship" in this passage (verse 9) remarks:

worship = do homage. Ap. 137.i.

Now by turning to Appendix 137 in the back, we can find not only the Greek word rendered "worship" in this passage (*proskuneō*) but also a brief, but complete, list of the various synonyms for worship in the New Testament.

The synonymous words for "worship" are listed as follows.

1. *proskuneō* = to prostrate one's self (in reverence), do homage; used, therefore, of the ACT of worship.

2. *sebomai* = to revere, to feel awe; used, therefore, of the INWARD FEELINGS (as No. 1 is of the outward act).

3. *sebazomai* = to be shy, or timid at doing anything. Occurs only in Rom. 1:25.

4. *latreuō* = to serve in official service (for hire, or reward); used of serving God in the externals of His worship.

5. *eusebeō* = to be pious or devout towards any one; to act with reverence, respect, and honor.

6. *therapeuō* = to wait upon, minister to (as a doctor does): hence, to heal; to render voluntary service and attendance, thus differing from No. 4.

The Newberry Reference Bible gives corrected readings and renderings of various King James Version words in brief marginal notes. It is quite valuable for the English reader in that, unlike the New Scofield and many other reference Bibles, the Greek word in question is always listed. For example, in James 3:1 the KJV text reads

My brethren, be not many masters, knowing that we shall receive the greater condemnation.

Newberry correctly points out that:

(1) the word "be" should be rendered "become"
(2) "masters" is more correctly "teachers"
(3) the word "the" is an addition by the translators and should be omitted
(4) "condemnation" is "judgment."

In each case the Greek words are listed for the reader's information and corroboration. The rendering, therefore, would be:

My brethren, become not many teachers, knowing that we shall receive greater judgment.

The meaning, of course, is that we should be cautious about becoming teachers without ample deliberation and preparation because teachers shall receive a closer examination because of their greater responsibility.

The greatest advantage of this work, however, lies in the area of Greek grammar, not vocabulary. Dr. F. F. Bruce, the great British Bible scholar, has remarked concerning the Newberry Bible that it is considered by many authorities to be "the most useful ... ever issued for English readers." We will make much more use of this study Bible in later chapters, when we arrive at our studies in Greek grammar.

Using Translations and Study Bibles Effectively

We have considered various works in these two categories and have examined their special features along with
examples illustrating their use. To gain the most use from
these works in regard to Greek words, however, the following suggestions may be helpful.

1. By using one of the concordances mentioned in the
last chapter in conjunction with translations, a great deal
more insight can be obtained into individual Greek words.
The definitions given for Greek words in these concordances are necessarily brief, but by finding the Greek word
which forms the basis of translation for a particular English
word in the King James Version and then comparing the
renderings of other translations, we can arrive at a fuller
and more contemporary meaning of the Greek word in
question.

For example, take the word rendered "set your affection" in Colossians 3:2 ("Set your affection on things above,
not on things on the earth"). First find the Greek verb
which is the basis for these three English words in the King
James Version; then compare this verse in a number of
modern versions (standard, study, and paraphrase) to discover more insight into what this Greek word actually
means.

2. Similarly, we can take the information on Greek words
supplied by various study Bibles and, by using the concordances, determine other places in the New Testament where
the particular Greek word appears. For example, Newberry tells us that the word rendered "verily" in John 1:51
(and several times in John's Gospel in the phrase "verily,
verily") is actually the Greek *amēn*. Now try tracing this
word *amēn* in the back of *Young's,* for example, to see

what other renderings this word receives in the KJV New Testament.

3. The notes regarding synonyms in various study Bibles can be amplified by comparing translations as well as the other occurrences of the words as shown in a concordance. For example, *teknon* and *huios* are two of several synonyms for "children," "sons," etc., in the New Testament (as we have seen in a previous example). Try tracing these words in *Strong's* or *Young's* and comparing them with the other synonyms shown. Also use modern translations to see the distinctions between the different Greek words in their contexts.

There are numerous possibilities for using these works both singly and together. As we learn about more Greek study aids in the following chapters, these two categories can be used in conjunction with these additional aids to enrich our understanding and appreciation of the Greek New Testament.

6

ENGLISH WORD STUDIES

In this chapter we will consider the remainder of those aids intended primarily for English readers. As with the previous aids, using them is quite simple and requires no detailed explanations. There are, however, some peculiar features of the different works which might be confusing and even discouraging to the reader who attempts to use them without a basic understanding of the nature of New Testament Greek and an acquaintance with the simpler aids already considered.

The works in this chapter can be divided generally into two broad categories: the first group, composed of one-volume works which offer studies in individual Greek words and vocabulary; the second group, made up of multivolume commentaries on the Greek text for English readers.

Bearing Burdens

Perhaps the best-known and most versatile example of the first group of aids is W. E. Vine's *Expository Dictionary of New Testament Words*. This work has been termed "one of the most valuable tools ever produced for the non-Greek reader." Other reviewers have stated that it is "indispensable to the pastor, teacher, or Bible student."

Vine's *Dictionary* is a standard work (it has been around for decades) and is the most comprehensive of the works in this first group. It is, in some ways, an English-Greek lexicon; that is, it lists English words (rather than Greek words) in the New Testament with almost as much completeness as a standard Greek lexicon.

Vine's *Dictionary* can be used without a concordance or any other tool. For example, let's take a puzzling passage which has confused many English readers:

> Bear ye one another's burdens, and so fulfill the law of Christ. For if a man thinks himself to be something, when he is nothing, he deceiveth himself. But let every man prove his own work, and then shall he have rejoicing in himself alone, and not in another. For every man shall bear his own burden (Galatians 6:2–5 KJV).

Here we have Paul telling us in verse 2 to bear one another's burdens but in verse 5 to bear our own burden. Is there a contradiction here? Apparently many people think so. For example, in the popular book, *Is THAT in the Bible?* by Dr. Charles F. Potter, there is a section on "Contradictions." Dr. Potter asks the question, "In what chapter does Paul contradict himself?" The answer he gives is,

> Galatians 6. In verse 2 Paul says "Bear ye one another's burdens, and so fulfill the law of Christ." In verse 5 he says "For every man shall bear his own burden."

Unfortunately, this book (like so many other secular treatments of religious subjects) is either not quite honest or else the author did not do his homework very well. The difficulty, as you may have guessed, exists only in the English text, not in the original Greek.

To solve this problem, let's find the entry "burden" in

Vine's *Dictionary*. In this work, the words are listed in alphabetical English order, usually according to the King James
Version. We find that Vine lists both nouns and verbs
under "burden." Here we are concerned with nouns. Under
Category A, therefore, we find the following definitions:

1. BAROS denotes a weight, anything pressing on one physi-
cally, Matt. 20:12, or that makes a demand on one's resources,
whether material, I Thess. 2:6 (to be burdensome), or spiritual,
Gal. 6:2;

2. PHORTION, lit., something carried (from *pherō,* to bear), is
always used metaphorically (except in Acts 27:10, of the lading
of a ship); of that which, though "light," is involved in disciple-
ship of Christ, Matt. 11:30; of that which will be the result, at the
judgment-seat of Christ, of each believer's work, Gal. 6:5.

Note: The difference between *phortion* and *baros* is that *phortion*
is simply something to be borne, without reference to its weight,
but *baros* always suggests what is heavy or burdensome. . . . Contrast *baros* in Gal. 6:2, with *phortion* in Ver. 5.

We see that Vine's *Dictionary* is arranged analytically, like
Young's Concordance. He does not simply list the words,
however; he gives brief but detailed explanations of them
as well. In the case of synonyms he also points out the
essential differences between the words.

By using *Vine's* alone, we can easily see the distinction
between the two words: in Galatians 6:2 *baros* is concerned
with the burdens of temptation and weakness which come
to every Christian. In 6:5 *phortion* refers to the load of work
or responsibility for which each Christian must answer
concerning himself. While you can help me with my infirmities, I am still responsible for my own service to the Lord
and will have to make an accounting one day (2 Corinthians 5:10). At that time it will do me no good to plead,
"Well, Mr. So-and-So did less work than I did," for we are

responsible for the "talents" (Matthew 25:14–30) and "pounds" (Luke 19:11–27) which the Lord gives *us,* not what he may give to someone else.

It can be seen that 'burden" is not incorrect in either case, but it is certainly confusing. Some modern versions clarify the passage to a certain extent by rendering 6:2 as "burdens" and 6:5 as "load" (see the New American Standard Bible and the New International Version). The full distinction, however, can be discovered only by using Greek study aids (such as Vine's *Dictionary*).

The Law: Our Schoolmaster?

William Barclay's *New Testament Words* is a small and inexpensive volume which provides a good introduction to New Testament words for the beginner. (This work will especially appeal to the many readers of Barclay's popular *Daily Study Bible*.). Barclay differs from Vine in that (1) the words are listed according to Greek rather than English words, and (2) the work is much shorter and selective, but (3) individual word studies are longer and more detailed.

One advantage of works such as this (for similar works, see Appendix C) is that we are not shown simply how the word is used in the New Testament (which we might find out ourselves through the use of concordances and other study aids) but also how it is used in classical and Hellenistic Greek. Barclay gives many examples of usage from both the papyri and the classical sources, most of which (in their Greek form) are certainly not available to the average Bible student. Actually, the writer of a word-study volume simply does most of the preliminary work and research for us and then gives us the benefit of his studies.

To consider this work, let's take another word often misunderstood and misrepresented, even in many modern versions. In Galatians 3:24 we read, "The Law has become our tutor to lead us to Christ" (NASB). This word "tutor" gives a meaning to the passage that is somewhat misleading, but which is practically unavoidable. By checking the King James Version we find "schoolmaster," which is no better. Barclay lists words according to the Greek, not the English (however, they are transliterated into English characters), so that we cannot simply find the word "schoolmaster" in the table of contents. We can either use a concordance to find the Greek word which lies behind "schoolmaster" and then find this particular study in the table of contents, or we can use the English index provided in the back of the volume. Doing the latter, we find "schoolmaster" and are informed of the page where this study is found. Turning to this page, we find that the Greek word in this case is *paidagōgos.*

Barclay defines *paidagōgos* as "the guardian of childhood's days." He remarks that "the word *paidagōgos* occurs in the New Testament in only two passages; but it is a word the correct understanding of which is essential, if Paul's thought is to be understood." He then lists several different contemporary translations of *paidagōgos,* but remarks that "none of these translations is fully satisfactory, for the very good reason that the *paidagōgos* carried out a function to which there is nothing precisely corresponding in our educational system."

Barclay then gives a detailed history of the function of the *paidagōgos* as gleaned from ancient history: "His duty was to accompany the boy to school each day and to see that he got there safely; to carry the boy's books and his lyre; to watch his conduct in school; to see to his conduct in the street; to train the boy in morals, in manners, and in deportment."

As an example of the research which backs up these word studies, Barclay gives the following quote from a classical source:

Socrates asks a youth: "And what does he [the *paidagōgos*] do with you?" The boy replies, "He takes me to my teachers."

As we can see from this word study, the *paidagōgos* was certainly not the equivalent of the modern "tutor" or "schoolmaster," even though our English word "pedagogy" is derived from this Greek word. In fact, no single English word could accurately represent this technical Greek term, and this fact illustrates the need to be able to make some use of Greek study aids in order to be able to correctly understand the background of the New Testament.

Words for Hell

Not all word-study volumes are so comprehensive in their explanation of Greek terms. Some merely provide basic information with references and leave it to the reader to follow up these references to determine for himself the peculiar force of the words in various passages. Such word-study volumes are particularly helpful in regard to Greek synonyms. W. E. Vine, by listing words under the English terms, is concerned primarily with Greek synonyms; Barclay, on the other hand, classifies according to the Greek words and is therefore more involved with English synonyms. This distinction generally holds true for most similar word-study volumes: those that classify according to English words consider the various Greek words which are rendered by this English word, and those that classify according to Greek words consider the various English words which render this Greek word.

For a good example of this type of approach to Greek synonyms, let's take the much-maligned and often-confusing word "hell." The tool we will use is Wuest's *Studies in the Vocabulary of the Greek New Testament for English Readers* (also contained in his *Word Studies in the Greek New Testament*). This small, inexpensive volume also makes a good introduction to the world of New Testament Greek words for the non-Greek reader. The work is similar to Vine's *Dictionary* in that words are listed by English rather than Greek form, but similar to Barclay's *New Testament Words* in that the work is briefer but with longer individual articles.

Under "hell," Wuest remarks:

There are three Greek words, each referring to a different place, all of which are translated by the one word *hell,* a fact that causes considerable confusion in interpreting the passages where they occur. These words are *geena, haides,* and *tartaroo.* The first comes into English in the word Gehenna, the second, in the word Hades, and the third, in the word Tartarus.

Gehenna refers to the final abode of the wicked dead, called the Lake of Fire in the Revelation (20:14–15). Where this word occurs, the translations should be hell. It is found in Mt. 5:22, 29–30; 10:28; 18:9; 23:15, 33; Mk. 9:43, 45, 47; Lk. 12:5; Jas. 3:6.

Haides refers to the temporary abode of the dead. . . .The word *haides* is from the Greek stem *id* which means "to see" and the Greek letter *Alpha* prefixed which makes the composite word mean "not to see," the noun meaning "the unseen." [The word occurs in] Mt. 11:23; 16:18; Lk. 10:15; 16:23; Acts 2:27, 31; Rev. 1:18; 6:8; 20:13–14.

Tartarus is the word in II Peter 2:4, "cast down to hell." The fallen angels were sent to their temporary prison base, *tartarus,* until the Great White Throne Judgment.

Thus we have the differences in these three words clearly pointed out, along with a list of the passages where they occur, all without any work on our part. If, as Wuest suggests "[you] make a study of these places where the word 'hell' occcurs, in the light of the distinctive Greek word found in each place, [you will] see how much better you understand these passages."

Jesus Christ: God or Man?

The second type of work in this chapter is the multivolume commentary on the Greek text for the non-Greek reader. Obviously, the approach to these works is somewhat different than for the above works. Here we cannot simply locate a particular English or Greek word alphabetically, since these word studies are arranged as verse-by-verse comments on the books of the New Testament.

The first and easiest way to use these works is simply as a commentary on any particular passage we might be studying. For our example, we will consider one of the great Christological passages and look at three of the most popular of these word-study sets.

Have this attitude in yourselves which was also in Christ Jesus, who, although He existed in the form of God, did not regard equality with God a thing to be grasped, but emptied Himself, taking the form of a bond-servant, and being made in the likeness of men. And being found in appearance as a man, He humbled Himself by becoming obedient to the point of death, even death on a cross (Philippians 2:5–8 NASB).

There are a number of questions connected with this

passage, but the one which first arrests the attention is the use of three different words, apparently synonyms. Christ was "in the form of God" (and took upon Himself "the form of a bond-servant"); He was made "in the likeness of men"; and He was found "in appearance as a man."

The question asked by the English reader is this: What is the basic and actual difference between these three words—"form," "likeness," and "appearance"? If we can find out exactly the shade of meaning of each of these words, we will discover a great deal about the nature of Christ.

1. *Form of God/Form of a Bondservant.* The first tool we will use is A. T. Robertson's *Word Pictures in the New Testament.* On this word "form," he remarks:

> *In the form of God (en morphēi theou).* Morphē means the essential attributes as shown in the form. In His preincarnate state Christ possessed the attributes of God and so appeared to those in Heaven who saw Him. Here is a clear statement by Paul of the deity of Christ. *Emptied himself (heauton ekenōse).* Of what did Christ empty Himself? Not of His divine nature. That was impossible. He continued to be the Son of God. . . .Undoubtedly Christ gave up His environment of glory. He took upon Himself the limitations of place (space), and of knowledge and of power, though still on earth retaining more of these than any mere man. He was without sin, though tempted as we are. "He stripped Himself of the insignia of majesty" (Lightfoot).

We might note in connection with this the comments by Bengel to the effect that "none could be in the form of God who was not God" (*New Testament Word Studies*).

2. *The Likeness of Men.* The next word is "likeness." For this example we will use Vincent's *Word Studies in the New Testament.* First he notes that the Greek word here is *homoiōma,* and then he remarks that the correct translation

of "was made" (KJV) is "becoming in." He then amplifies this as follows:

> Notice the choice of the verb, not *was,* but *became: entered into* a new state. *Likeness* . . . does not imply the reality of our Lord's humanity, as *form* implied the reality of His deity. That fact is stated in "the form of a servant.". . . "*Likeness* of men" expresses the fact that His mode of manifestation *resembled* what men are. This leaves room for the assumption of another side of His nature—the *divine*—in the likeness of which He did not appear. As He appeared to men, He was like themselves, with a *real* likeness; but this likeness to men did not express His *whole* self. The *totality* of His being could not appear to men, for that *involved* the form of God. . . .He was not *identical* with men, because there was an element of His personality which did not dwell in them— equality with God. . . ."To affirm likeness is at once to assert *similarity* and to deny *sameness*" (Dickson).

We can already see therefore a real and important difference between "form" and "likeness"—one implies identity while the other implies similarity.

3. *Appearance As a Man.* For the consideration of our third word, we will look at Kenneth S. Wuest's *Word Studies in the Greek New Testament for the English Reader.* Since this work is slightly different from the first two, we will examine its features a little more closely. This work (one of the most popular of the word-study sets, and one of the simplest to understand for the non-Greek reader) is actually a collection of sixteen shorter books on the Greek New Testament (these sixteen volumes are still available separately). A number of these utilize the same basic method found in the first two works considered—i.e., a verse-by-verse consideration of the Greek New Testament. Approximately half the books of the New Testament are considered in this fashion. In contrast to the above, however,

Wuest also includes his own expanded translation along with his comments on these books. In addition to these commentaries, Wuest also includes a number of topical and vocabulary studies (including the *Vocabulary* previously considered). Wuest (like Robertson, but unlike Vincent) gives the Greek words in English characters.

In this section we are concerned with the commentary portion of the three-volume set. Wuest's comments on "appearance" are:

The word (*schēma*) is the translation of a Greek word that refers to an outward expression that is assumed from the outside and does not come from within. The word . . . referred to that which is purely outward, and appeals to the senses. Our Lord's humanity was real. He was really a Man, but He was not a real man in the sense that He was like others of the human race, only a man. He was always in His incarnation more than man. There was always that single personality with a dual nature. His deity did not make Him more or less than a Man, and His humanity did not make Him less than absolute Deity. But He was not found in fashion as *a* man. The indefinite article should not be in the translation. He was found in outward guise as man, not *a* man. He was not a man but God, although He had assumed human nature yet without sin.

Wuest supplies at the end of his comments a translation of this verse:

And being found to be in outward guise as man, He stooped very low, having become obedient to the extent of death, even such a death as that upon a cross.

This important passage in Philippians 2 teaches us that Christ was truly God and also truly humble. He was in the form (*morphē*) of God and took upon Himself the form (*morphē*) of a servant.

Christ also became in the likeness of men in general. There was a similarity—indeed, many similarities—between Him and mankind. He grew tired, He grew hungry, He grew thirsty (see John 4: 6–8, etc.). But at the same time there were essential differences as well. Christ was still God, even when here in the flesh. This is something that could be said about no other man. It is interesting to note that on the Mount of Transfiguration the three disciples saw Christ's true essence shine forth as His human appearance was momentarily laid aside. The word rendered "transfigured" (Matthew 17:2) is *metamorphoōmai*, which derives from *morphē*. This tells us that Christ wasn't simply *changed* from one thing to another but that His outward appearance momentarily reflected His true inner nature.

Finally, Christ was found "in appearance as a man." He assumed the "guise" or outward appearance of one single human being (by means of the incarnation, of course) so that from outward appearance alone (see Matthew 16:17) one could not have told that Christ was truly the Son of God. He was truly a man, but He always remained *more* than just man, for he was the God-Man, "God With Us" (Matthew 1:23).

As God, Christ is "able to save forever those who draw near to God through Him" (Hebrews 7:25 NASB). Yet as Man we realize that He is "One who has been tempted in all things as we are, yet without sin" (Hebrews 4:15 NASB) and is therefore able to sympathize with our temptations and infirmities and eager to help us if we "draw near with confidence to the throne of grace" (Hebrews 4:16 NASB). Christ is both our Saviour and our Succorer, both our Sacrifice and our Great High Priest.

Two Words for Temple

Suppose, however, that we are not interested in any particular passage but simply in discovering more insight into a specific word or words. Since the above works are arranged as commentaries, how can we find any particular Greek or English word study in a brief amount of time? We can first look at our concordances to see where a particular English word occurs, then look at the commentary on any of these passages. However, there is one procedure which might help us to gain the most information in the least time. Generally these works present the most complete studies of any particular word at the first occurrence of the word in the New Testament. Where there are exceptions to this rule, the reader is usually referred to the passage which contains the most complete explanation.

For example, let's take the English word "temple" and discover the Greek word or words from which this word is derived. By using any concordance, we see that the first time "temple" is used in the New Testament is in Matthew 4:5. Now locating this passage in Vincent's *Word Studies,* for example, we find the following:

The word *temple (hieron,* lit. *sacred place)* signifies the whole compass of the sacred inclosure, with its porticoes, courts, and other subordinate buildings; and should be carefully distinguished from the other word, *naos,* also rendered temple, which means the temple itself—the "Holy Place" and the "Holy of Holies." When we read, for instance, of Christ teaching in the temple *(hieron)* we must refer it to one of the temple porches. So it is from the *hieron,* the court of the Gentiles, that Christ expels the money-changers and cattle-merchants. In Matthew 27:51, it is the veil of the *naos* which is rent. . . . In the account of Zecharias entering into the *temple of the Lord* to burn incense (Luke 1:9), the word is *naos,* the holy place in which the altar of incense stood.

It is important to keep this distinction in mind as we study the New Testament; to use one word where the other should be used would be inappropriate and confusing.

It is also instructive to notice that Christ, not being a priest of the tribe of Levi, never entered into the temple building itself (*naos*) but is connected in Scripture only with the *hieron*. Yet Christ describes His physical body as a *naos* (John 2:19–21) and the Church (as His "body") as *naos* (1 Corinthians 3:16).

Despite the fact that the One for whom the temple was actually built was not allowed to enter it, yet Christ has entered into the *true* "holy place" in Heaven and there serves as our Great High Priest to continually make intercession for us (see Hebrews 4:14–15; 7:25; 9:24).

Hints for Further Study

The use of the study aids described in this chapter is seen to be simple and obvious. They can be used by anyone, no matter how much or little New Testament Greek he knows and no matter how many other aids he may or may not have. For those who do have such aids as the concordances mentioned in Chapter Four, these word-study books can be of even more benefit.

1. For example, we may find a word that interests us by using *Strong's*, *Young's*, or a similar concordance, and we may desire to obtain more information about this word than the brief notes in these works give us. We can turn to one of the word-study aids mentioned in this chapter to discover more insight into such words. The word found in Romans 8:29–30 and rendered "predestinate" (KJV) is a good example to try.

2. In contrast, we might read of a particular Greek word in a word-study book and desire to see exactly where this word appears in the New Testament, in what contexts, and how it is rendered. This can be done by referring to *Strong's* or an analytical concordance. For example, after reading about the Greek word *kardia* ("heart," as in John 14:1) in *Vincent's, Robertson's,* or a similar word-study volume, try using a concordance to see where this word appears in the New Testament and in what contexts.

3. In the area of Barclay's *New Testament Words* (and other works classified according to Greek rather than English words) we can use one of the already-mentioned concordances to discover the Greek word which lies behind a particular English word, and then easily locate this word in the table of contents. For example, there are two primary Greek words rendered "good" in the New Testament. Barclay considers one of these words. First find the Greek words translated "good," then see which of these words Barclay considers, then read his study of the word.

These suggestions can be enlarged and adapted to fit any similar word-study volumes. Comparing the information given on particular Greek words in these volumes with the various renderings of English translations as given in the last chapter can also be quite illuminating in your study of the world's greatest Book—the Greek New Testament.

7

LEXICONS AND

GREEK-ENGLISH CONCORDANCES

All of the works which we have previously discussed are intended primarily for the use of the English reader. Now we are ready to consider works that are actually designed with the Greek reader and student in mind. The aids we will study in this chapter and the next are basic tools for the Greek scholar, pastor, teacher, writer, professor, and seminary student. Yet with only a small amount of effort the non-Greek reader can learn to use these tools and thereby enrich his own study of the New Testament.

The Lexicons

The most basic tools for the Greek reader are undoubtedly the lexicons. We have explained that a lexicon is a word book, a dictionary of Greek words. There are three types of lexicons designed for the student of the Greek New Testament, and we will consider examples from each type or category. The basic procedure for locating a Greek word remains the same, however, with any of these lexicons. How can the English reader learn to use these scholarly works?

1. First of all, this can be accomplished by using certain shortcuts rather than the standard procedure used by Greek readers. There are a number of works designed with the non-Greek reader in mind. For example, an edition of *Thayer's Greek Lexicon* is now available which is keyed to the numbers in *Strong's Concordance,* so that if you own a *Strong's* it is a simple matter to locate a Greek word by first locating the number of the word in the concordance and then matching the number in the lexicon. Another such "number-keyed" work is Ralph Winter's *Word Study New Testament.* This is a two-volume set with a King James New Testament in one volume which is keyed to the *Englishman's Greek-English Concordance* in the other volume. The latter is keyed to Arndt and Gingrich's *Greek Lexicon* and Kittel's *Theological Dictionary of the New Testament.*

2. However, the best (and in the long run, the simplest) method is to master the simple procedure used by the Greek reader. This requires nothing more than becoming slightly acquainted with the letters and order of the Greek alphabet. Learning to do this is well worth the effort for several reasons: it will save you time later on when using Greek lexicons, as you do not have to first consult a concordance or an index; and many of the most valuable lexicons, as well as other aids, do not contain shortcut methods or indices, so that the student who is dependent on such shortcuts will not be able to use these important works.

This ability to locate Greek words in a Greek lexicon will be of great help as you continue your studies of New Testament Greek through the use of other aids. The average Bible student with no previous knowledge of the Greek alphabet can generally locate a Greek word in less than five minutes the first time. Each time it is done will decrease the time period somewhat, until soon the English reader will be flipping through the pages of the lexicon with the ease of a Greek scholar!

The Standard Lexicon

For our first example in using a lexicon, we will take a standard tool: the *Greek-English Lexicon to the Greek New Testament and Other Early Christian Literature* (translated from the German of W. Bauer by W. F. Arndt and F. W. Gingrich). There are three reasons for using this work for these examples. First, it is the most up-to-date standard work currently available for New Testament Greek. Secondly, it is easily available at most bookstores and many libraries (many pastors also have a copy). Thirdly, it is the work most often quoted today by Biblical writers and expositors and therefore the one work which the average reader is most likely to encounter in his day-to-day reading. William Barclay, the popular Bible expositor, has described this work as "completely indispensable to the student of the language of the New Testament."

If a person can make use of one such lexicon, he can make use of *any* standard lexicon. Therefore if a reader already owns or has access to a Greek lexicon, the same procedures as outlined below will apply (except for page numbers).

Step One. The first step before locating a Greek word is to determine the Greek form (that is, in Greek characters) of the word which we desire to locate. In order to find this word in the standard lexicon, the word *must* be in the basic or "dictionary" position. The Greek student would simply look at his Greek New Testament, see the words which are used, mentally determine the root or dictionary position, and then locate the word in the lexicon. This would take only a few moments. For the English reader the procedure is not as fast, but the results are exactly the same. The simplest method of determining the Greek word in Greek characters in basic position of any particular English word is to use a *Strong's, Young's,* or other analytical concordance. Another method is to use a word-study volume which lists the Greek form of a word (as some of those mentioned in the last chapter). Vine's *Dictionary* is a good example of a work which does this. However, it should be pointed out that not all of these works list Greek words in their dictionary form, and this could prove confusing to the beginner. For convenience, therefore, it is best to use a work such as *Vine's* or one of the concordances which *always* list Greek words in this basic form.

For our first example, let's take two words which we have already consulted in Vine's *Dictionary*: the two words rendered "burden" in Galatians 6. Note first that these two words, *baros* and *phortion,* are written in Greek characters as βαρος and φορτιον.

Step Two. Next we locate the word in the lexicon. The primary—indeed, the only—real difficulty in using a lexicon is the fact that the Greek words are listed in alphabetical order according to Greek characters. This difficulty exists for the average reader because of his unfamiliarity with the Greek characters.

Don't be frightened by these strange symbols: it is *not* necessary to memorize the Greek alphabet in order to use a Greek lexicon. Though a little slower, it is quite possible and fairly simple to find an entry simply by referring to a chart of the Greek alphabet as given in Appendix B of this book (also found in the preface to *Gall's Concordance*; preceding the Greek dictionary in *Strong's Concordance*; and in many dictionaries, encyclopedias, etc.). After using this method for a couple of dozen times, you will find that you are learning the Greek alphabet the painless way, and that you almost automatically turn to the proper entry.

For convenience, we suggest that you copy out the chart of the Greek alphabet as given in this book and paste or insert it in the front of the lexicon that you are using. Along with this, you might first go through your lexicon and write down on your chart the pages on which each section dealing with a different letter of the alphabet begins. This will save time at first in thumbing through the lexicon trying to find the particular Greek letter which begins a word. You will find yourself using this chart less and less until soon you will not need to use it at all.

First, let's take the word *baros* (βαρος). This word is quite simple to locate. The "b" (beta) and the "a" (alpha) should pose no problem. Notice that in the Greek form what looks like "p" in Greek (rho) is actually equal to "r" in English. Note carefully, also, the difference between "o" (omicron) and "ō" (omega, which is ω in Greek). Also note that the letter sigma has two forms: *s* when it occurs at the end of a word, as it does here, and σ when it occurs elsewhere.

First we need to locate the section in the lexicon which deals with words beginning with letter beta. Note that this letter (like the English "b") is the second letter in the alphabet, coming immediately after alpha ("a"). (It is interesting that our own word "alphabet" comes from the names of the first two letters of the Greek alphabet—alpha and beta.) In the unabridged Arndt and Gingrich *Lexicon* (from which we will be quoting in this example; there is also an abridged version available—see Appendix C), the listing for beta begins on page 129. The next letter in *baros* is alpha. This means that *baros* will be found near the first part of the beta listing. The third letter is rho, which (as in the English "r") follows "p" (Greek pi). *Bar-* begins on page 132. The fourth letter is omicron. This "o" follows "n" (Greek nu; note that it looks like the English "v"; note also that what looks like "n" in Greek is actually eta, written "ē"). The words beginning *baro-* begin on page 133. The final letter is sigma. This letter is not actually needed to locate the word, however, as there is only one listing for *baro-* and this is the word we are seeking: *baros.* The word is found on page 133, column two, entry one.

Now for the definition: the basic meaning is given as "weight, burden, only figurative." This means that in the authorities and ancient sources consulted for the prepara-tion of this lexicon, the word *baros* is found only in a figurative and never in a literal sense.

The simple definition of *baros* is further amplified as follows:

  I.   *burden* of the day's work (Matt. 20:12); of temptations (Gal. 6:2)
       to impose a burden on someone (Rev. 2:24)
       an unweighed burden
 II.   *weight* of influence which someone enjoys or claims;
       wield authority, insist on one's importance (I Thess. 2:6)
III.   *fulness,* an *everlasting fulness of glory* (II Cor. 4:17)

You will find the verse we have been considering listed under definition number one: "*burden* of temptations." (You will notice also that the many references to extrabib-lical literature and sources have been omitted in this quote.) We find therefore that we are to help bear one another's "weaknesses or infirmities." This fact is also revealed to us in Romans 15:1:

Now we who are strong ought to bear the weaknesses of those without strength, and not just please ourselves (NASB).

Step Three. Now let's find the word *phortion* (φορτιον). This word is a little more difficult, but the procedure is exactly the same. First notice that "ph" in English is actually one letter in Greek: phi (pronounced "f" as in "fight") and is found near the end of the alphabet. Again, notice the "n" (nu) and be sure not to confuse it with the English "v" or the Greek eta (which resembles an English "n").

Step Four. (1) The section for phi begins on page 859; (2) *pho-* words begin on page 870; (3) words beginning with *phor-* on page 872; (4) *phort-* also on page 872, as are (5) *phorti-* words; (6) and *phortion* is the first entry on page 873. The definition is given as "burden, load." This is further amplified as follows:

I. Literally of the *cargo* of a ship;
II. Symbolically of the oppressive *burden* of the law (Matt. 23:4); Gal. 6:5; everyone is to concern himself about his own burden, rather than to compare himself complacently with others.

This study of *baros* and *phortion* brings out the same distinction we have already observed: *baros* is concerned with "burdens" of temptation and weakness, and *phortion* with "burdens" of responsibility and duty.

The Papyri-Based Lexicon

The best example of a lexicon in this category is the *Vocabulary of the Greek New Testament,* by Moulton and Milligan. This classic work is based on the thousands of papyri which have been discovered during the past decades. By examining papyri, the authors have compiled a lexicon which not only defines most of the Greek words found in the New Testament, but also gives illustrations of their use in ordinary writing, business, and everyday affairs during the early Christian (and, in some cases, pre-Christian) era.

As with other lexicons, this work is listed in alphabetical Greek order. The procedure for locating a word is therefore exactly the same as with the Arndt and Gingrich *Lexicon* already considered. This is one of the reasons why it is important for anyone interested in using Greek study aids to master this method of locating words according to the Greek alphabet: this is a standard procedure which can be used with dozens of types of reference works.

Step One. For our example with this tool, we will take another word with which we are familiar: *teleios,* the word rendered "perfect" in Philippians 3:15. By consulting one of the tools we have considered previously, we find that this word in Greek is τελειος.

Step Two. First, looking at the alphabet table, note tau ("t") and be sure to distinguish from theta ("th"). Note that tau is found near the end of the alphabet (and therefore near the end of the lexicon), in contrast to theta (which does not appear in this word, of course), which is found near the beginning. Also notice that both of the "e's" are epsilon, not eta. The other letters are already familiar to us from the previous example.

Step Three. (1) We find by turning through the lexicon (an index of the first page of each letter of the alphabet can also be made for this work if the student has access to the work) that the tau section begins on page 624. As in English, tau ("t") follows sigma ("s") and precedes upsilon ("u"). (2) Note that *te* begins on page 627; (3) words beginning *tel* on page 629; and (4) the first word listed as *tel* is the word for which we are searching: *teleios.*

We see that the basic definition is given as, "Literally, 'having reached its end.' Hence, (1) 'full-grown,' 'mature.' " The greatest advantage of this lexicon, however, lies in its abundant quotes and extracts from various ancient documents and writings.

For example, when referring to persons, *teleios* is used of "heirs being of age" and is also found in the sentence, "all proving that women who have attained maturity are mistresses of their persons, and can remain with their husbands or not as they choose." This sentiment, expressed in A.D. 186, might find sympathetic acceptance among many women today!

The word is also used of animals, as, for example, "four full-grown cocks" in a reference from A.D. 137.

When used of inanimate objects, *teleios* means "in good working order or condition," as, for example, "one perfect Theban mill," "fourteen acacia-trees in good condition," or "a complete lampstand."

We also have a petition of a physician to the Praefect asking to be relieved from certain public duties on the ground of his profession (ca. A.D. 140). He requests "that complete exemption from compulsory services be granted to persons practicing the profession of physician." Here the word rendered "complete" is *teleios*.

The meaning and usage of the word in ordinary language is thus readily determined. The meaning in Philippians 3:15 is seen to be "mature" in the Christian life as opposed to "babes in Christ" (1 Corinthians 3:1-2) and does not refer at all to "sinless perfection," to one who never sins or makes a mistake. We might compare this illustration with the admonitions to three classes of Christians in 1 John 2:13: fathers, young men, little children (literally, young children under instruction or of school age: the

Greek word is *paidia,* with which compare *paidagōgos* in Chapter Six. The word in 1 John 2:12 is *teknia* or "born-ones").

The Theological Lexicon

The third type of lexicon we will consider is the theological lexicon, one which is not concerned simply with philological definitions and illustrations of words, but also with the consideration of how these words are actually used in the New Testament and with the various shades of meaning which they exhibit in different contexts.

Perhaps the best-known example of this type of lexicon is the *Biblico-Theological Lexicon of New Testament Greek,* by Hermann Cremer. Certain peculiar features of this work need to be explained. The present edition of this work (the fourth, which dates from 1886) contains a regular lexicon section which is listed according to Greek alphabetical order, as with any other lexicon. However, there is a supplement which is almost as large as the original section and which contains additional word-study articles added since the original edition. In this supplement the words are *not* consistently in alphabetical order. In order to use this work, therefore, the student must refer to the index provided in the back of the book. This index lists *all* the words considered in the lexicon (both in the main section and in the supplement) and the page number on which the entries occur. This actually facilitates locating a particular word for the English reader (even though the words are listed in their Greek form) because we do not have to flip through the pages of the entire lexicon to find our entry, but can simply scan the list.

This lexicon considers almost every word in the New Testament of any theological importance, but it does not consider every single word, as does the standard lexicon.

Step One. For our example using this work, let's take the word "liberty" as found in Romans 8:21:

The creature itself also shall be delivered from the bondage of corruption into the glorious liberty of the children of God (KJV).

Tracing this English word in one of the tools previously considered, we see that there are several Greek words rendered "liberty" (in the KJV), but one word is used more than all the others combined. This word is *eleutheria,* which is also the word found in this passage in Romans 8. In Greek this word is spelled ἐλευθερια.

Step Two. (1) Note that the word begins with epsilon ("e"). (2) Also note the letter theta ("th"), which is two letters in English, but only one letter in Greek. The other letters are already familiar to us.

Step Three. (1) Turning now to the index in Cremer's *Lexicon,* we find that the section listing epsilon words begins on the fourth page of the index. (2) Note that *el* comes after *ek* and before *en.* (3) Finding the *el* section, we note that *eleu* comes after *eleo* and *ell.* (4) We find that our word, *eleutheria,* is the first word listed in the *eleu* section, and that the entry for this word is found on page 251.

Step Four. Turning now to page 251, we find Cremer's definition as follows:

Eleutheria, freedom, independence, in social and national life; usually denoting the absence of all limitations to independent action, *to be Lord and Master of oneself,* I Cor. 10:29. Freedom is a distinctive blessing of the economy of grace, which, in contrast with the Old Testament economy, is represented as including independence of legal restraints and rules of life, Gal. 2:4, 5:1,13; or, in contrast with the present subjection of the creature to the bondage of corruption, as the future state of the children of God, Rom. 8:21. . . . Whatever be the definitive form it assumes in the varying relations of life, we must take Christian freedom to denote the one essential and comprehensive result of redemption, the correlative of life; for it is not only freedom from the consequences of sin, but (if we may use the expression) *it restores the man to himself,* makes him his own master, independent of every power alien to his higher nature,—of sin in all its forms and consequences,—and guarantees for him unhindered possession and unfettered action of his life in a manner conformable to his real self.

Such a work as this presents much more information on individual words than is possible with other types of lexicons. Of course the comments are personal and are not to be taken as definitive. While the reader may not always agree with the remarks of such works, he will certainly benefit from the insight and scholarship of the author.

The reader who has access to this work (and the previous works) will note that these entries are obviously intended for the Greek scholar. They contain much information and many quotes in Greek, which cannot be read by the English reader (and which we have deleted in these examples). This is why Vincent remarked in his preface to *Word Studies in the New Testament:* "Can the reader who knows no Greek be put in possession of these treasures [of the Greek New Testament]? Not of all." (See Chapter Three.) However, as Vincent acknowledges, the average reader can obtain, use, and benefit from the basic definitions and gist of the studies provided in these scholarly works.

Greek-English Concordances

A companion tool to the standard lexicon is the Greek or Greek-English concordance. We have already discussed the English-Greek concordance, which lists English words and then shows the various passages where these English words occur and the Greek words from which they are translated. However, for the advancing student who has learned to locate words in a standard lexicon, the Greek-English concordance may be more valuable and more convenient than the other type of concordance.

The Greek concordance (the standard work in this area is Moulton and Geden's *Concordance to the Greek New Testament*) lists the words of the Greek New Testament and the passages where they occur in the actual form in which they occur in the New Testament. This work is not easily usable by the English reader. The Greek-English concordance, on the other hand, lists Greek words alphabetically according to the Greek alphabet (just as a lexicon does) but underneath each entry lists *in English* the passages where these words occur. The advantage of this work is in determining English synonyms—i.e., listing the various passages in the New Testament where a particular Greek word occurs, along with the various renderings of the word. This type of concordance is based on the Greek words in the Greek text rather than on the English words in the English version. It is therefore less misleading than the simple English or English-Greek concordance.

The two most popular works in this category are the *Englishman's Greek Concordance* and J. B. Smith's *Greek-English Concordance*. Both are based on the King James Version. The *New Englishman's Greek Concordance* (Associated Publishers and Authors) is also available. This work is keyed to the numbers in *Strong's Concordance,* and the procedure for locating words in this work is exactly the same as with the *New Thayer's Greek Lexicon* (mentioned above). For the other two works, entries can be located in the identical manner as with any standard lexicon.

Since we have already considered this procedure in detail, we will not belabor the point here, but simply give an example illustrating the usefulness of such works. One of their advantages is that they show us plainly and conveniently all the occurrences of a given Greek word in the order in which it occurs in the New Testament.

For example, let's take several of the words rendered "worship" which we have considered in Chapter Five and see some of the passages where these words occur and how they are rendered. For our example we will use the *Englishman's Greek Concordance.* However, since both works are based on the King James Version, the results would be the same with either of the two works mentioned.

1. *Proskuneō.* First notice the Greek form of the word: προσκυνεω. Next locate the section for words beginning with pi, then *pr, pro, pros,* etc. Under *proskuneō* you will notice some sixty entries. Checking these carefully, you will find that the word is always rendered by some form of "worship." A few examples of this are as follows:

> Matt. 2:2,8,11: (of the "Wise Men" *worshipping* the infant Christ)
> Matt. 4:9: "if thou wilt fall down and *worship* me"
> Matt. 28:9: "they came and held Him by the feet, and *worshipped* Him"
> Heb. 1:6: "and let all the angels of God *worship* Him"
> Rev. 4:10: "*worship* Him that liveth for ever and ever"

2. *Sebomai.* Notice the Greek form of this word σεβομαι. Locate the word as above and compare the renderings. A few examples follow:

Matt. 15:9: "but in vain do they *worship* Me"
Acts 13:43: "many of the Jews and *religious* proselytes"
Acts 17:17: "he disputed with the Jews, and with the *devout* persons"

3. *Latreuō* (λατρευω). Some occurrences are:

Matt. 4:10: "(God) only shalt thou *serve*"
Luke 1:74: "that we . . . might *serve* Him without fear"
Acts 24:14: "so *worship* I the God of my fathers"
Rom. 1:9: "God is my witness, whom I *serve* with my spirit"
Heb. 9:9 "gifts and sacrifices that could not make him that *did the service* perfect"
Heb. 10:2: "the *worshippers* once purged should have had no more conscience of sins"

4. *Eusebeō*. This word is found twice in the New Testament. The Greek form is ευσεβεω. In addition to Acts 17:23, see:

I Tim. 5:4: "let them learn first to *shew piety* at home"

5. *Therapeuō* (Θεραπευω). Notice from the occurrences of the word that the main meaning of *therapeuō* is "to cure or heal," being rendered "worship" only once. A few examples are:

Matt. 4:23: "*healing* all manner of sickness"
Matt. 17:16: "I brought him . . . and they could not *cure* him"
Luke 7:21: "he *cured* many of their infirmities"
Acts 17:25: "neither is *worshipped* with men's hands"

Suggestions for Further Study

Using these works requires knowing (1) the Greek word which lies behind a particular English word, and (2) the basic or dictionary form of the word in the original Greek characters. At this point in our studies we cannot determine these facts from the Greek New Testament itself, and therefore it is necessary for us to make use of other aids in conjunction with the ones considered in this chapter. We have already seen how this can be done in relation to concordances and certain word-study volumes. In later chapters we will learn how to work directly from the Greek New Testament itself. For those readers who have access to works such as the ones considered in this and previous chapters, the following are suggested for further study:

1. *psuchē*, the common word for "soul" in the New Testament.
2. *stephanos* and *diadēma*, two words for "crown."
3. *aphthartos*, rendered "immortal" in 1 Timothy 1:17.
4. *anakainōsis*, rendered "renewing" in Romans 12:2.
5. *epistrēpho*, the common word for "convert."
6. the ninefold "fruit of the Spirit" in Galatians 5:22–23.
7. the three words for "redeem": *agorazō, exagorazō, lutroō*.

Try locating these words first in a concordance or other work to determine the Greek spelling, then in any of the tools considered in this chapter to see what light these standard Greek tools shed on these important New Testament words.

8

GREEK WORD STUDIES

In this chapter we will look briefly at some study aids which are in some ways the counterparts of those discussed in Chapter Six. In that chapter we looked at word-study volumes which were intended for, or easily used by, the average non-Greek reader. In this chapter we will consider word-study sets and volumes designed especially for the Greek reader and student.

As in the former case, we can divide this category of aids into two groups: works concerned with individual Greek words in the New Testament; and commentaries on the Greek text of the New Testament. What is the difference between these works and those previously considered? In these works, the Greek words are almost always presented in their original form and characters, and many times these words are not even translated into English, as the author assumes that the reader is familiar with Greek. In addition, there are often copious quotes from the Greek New Testament as well as from other Biblical languages (such as Hebrew and Syriac), classical sources, and (particularly in the case of older works) scholarly languages, such as Latin, French, and German.

Can the English reader really make use of these works? Yes, though he cannot expect to derive the full benefit of them, nor can he expect to proceed as swiftly and easily as the Greek reader when using them.

Things New and Old

We will keep our example in this chapter brief in view of the fact that the average reader may have less access to these scholarly works (though they are standard works and available in many bookstores and libraries) and will probably use such works less than those discussed in previous chapters.

One of the most popular works in the area of individual word studies is *Synonyms of the New Testament,* by Richard C. Trench. The late Wilbur M. Smith remarked concerning this work that "once one becomes accustomed to using this book, he will find himself continually referring to it when desiring to distinguish accurately between the different shades of meaning of more or less similar New Testament Greek words." As the title indicates, this work is concerned with Greek synonyms—different Greek words which are similar but not identical in meaning. It is considered to be practically definitive in regard to those words which it considers.

Trench has studies on over two hundred words in over one hundred separate articles. In the table of contents, however, these words are listed in no particular order, and the student who desires to locate a particular Greek word must make use of the alphabetical index to Greek words found in the back of the book. Locating a particular Greek word in this index is exactly the same as locating a word in a lexicon as discussed in the last chapter.

Step One. For our example, let's take the English word

"new." By making use of a concordance or other tool, we learn that there are two Greek words for "new" in the New Testament: *neos* and *kainos*. The Greek forms of these words are *νεος* and *καινος*.

Step Two. Turning to the index, we can choose either of these two words to locate. In either case we would be referred to page 219.

Step Three. Turning to page 219, we find a detailed, six-page study of these two synonyms. Reading through this article carefully, the English reader will find that there is only a small amount of text which he must skip over for one reason or another. Most of the article can be easily understood simply by keeping in mind the Greek forms of the two main words involved, *neos* and *kainos*. What we must omit will be found to detract only slightly from our overall understanding of these two words.

Trench remarks concerning *neos* and *kainos* that "some have denied that any difference can in the New Testament be traced between these two words" and he does show places where the words seem to be used interchangeably: e.g.:

new (*neos*) man (Colossians 3:10) and new (*kainos*) man (Ephesians 2:15)

new (*neos*) covenant (Hebrews 12:24) and new (*kainos*) covenant (Hebrews 9:15)

new (*neos*) wine (Matthew 9:17) and new (*kainos*) wine (Matthew 26:29).

Trench proves by a careful study, however, that the words are not exact counterparts. "The same covenant may be qualified as *neos,* or *kainos,* as it is contemplated from one point of view or another. So too the same man, or the same wine, may be *neos* or *kainos,* or it may be both; but a different notion is predominant according to the one epithet applied or the other."

Basically, Trench illustrates the distinguishing difference between the two words as follows: "Contemplate the new under aspects of *time,* as that which has recently come into existence, and this is *neos.* . . . But contemplate the new, not now under aspects of time, but of *quality,* the new, as set over against that which has seen service, the outworn, the effete or marred through age, and this is *kainos.*"

It is in pointing out such careful, and sometimes minute, distinctions as these that Trench excels. Such word studies go far beyond the range of a lexicon.

Other works concerned with individual words include the *Theological Dictionary of the New Testament* and the *New International Dictionary of New Testament Theology.* The former work is arranged according to Greek words, the latter according to English words, but both are concerned with the original language of the New Testament in terms of the theological import and connotations of the original words. The former work (known widely as "Kittel's," after one of the editors) is probably the most comprehensive and scholarly study of New Testament words presently available. Though definitely not of a conservative slant, this work can provide much information of a technical nature for the careful and discriminating Bible student.

Think on These Things

In the second group of aids, we have commentaries on the Greek New Testament. Many such works have been published in the past, but there are two main works still in print today and easily obtainable by the English reader (and which comment on the entire New Testament: for works concerned with individual books only, see Appendix C). These are *The Expositor's Greek Testament,* edited by W. Robertson Nicoll, and *Alford's Greek Testament.* We will take one brief example from each work, though the format of these two works is identical.

Step One. As with the commentaries in Chapter Six, the easiest way to use these works is simply to locate the comments on a particular passage which we are studying. For our example, let's take Philippians 4:8, Paul's list of criteria of worthy objects for our consideration and medi- tation, a passage of immense importance in our daily lives as Christians.

Finally, brethren, whatever is true, whatever is honorable, whatever is right, whatever is pure, whatever is lovely, whatever is of good repute, if there is any excellence and if anything worthy of praise, let your mind dwell on these things (NASB).

We will use for this example *Alford's Greek Testament.* To use such works as these it is helpful to be able to recognize the names of the books of the New Testament in their Greek form. This is usually quite simple to do at a glance, as they are quite similar to the English forms (e.g., Philip- pians—ΦΙΛΙΠΠΗΣΙΟΥΣ). However, this is not absolutely essential, since it is a simple matter to find the beginning of the section on Philippians (page 152) by flipping through the pages of the volume. By glancing at the top of the page, we can easily find the comments dealing with chapter 4, verse 8 (on page 190).

Step Two. We will notice at the top of this page the Greek text of verse 8 (and part of verse 9). Underneath we have the comments on this verse, the gist of which is given below (note the many Greek words as you read, but do not worry about them at this point):

This beautiful sentence, full of the apostle's fervor and elo-
quence, derives much force from the frequent repetition of *hosa,*
and then of *ei tis. alēthē*—subjective, *truthful:* not *true* in matter
of fact. The whole regards ethical qualities. *semna*—it is difficult
to give it in any one English word: *honest* and *honorable* are too
weak; *revered* and *venerable, grave* are seldom applied to *things.*
Nor do I know any other more eligible. *dikaia*—not *just,* in
respect of others merely—but *right,* in that wider sense in which
dikaiosunē is used—before God and man: see this sense Acts
10:22; Romans 5:7. *hagna*—not merely *chaste* in the ordinary
confined acceptation: but *pure* generally. *prosphilē*—lovely, in
the most general sense ... the exhortation is markedly and
designedly as *general* as possible. *euphēma*—again, general,
and with reference to general fame: *of good report. ei tis aretē*
... sums up all of which have gone before and generalizes still
further.

Don't be confused and discouraged by the large number
of Greek words (presented in this quote in their transliterated forms, of course). How can we understand this passage? (1) Notice, first of all, that in most of the cases Alford
defines the words in English immediately after listing the
word. (2) In those cases where he does not do so, we can
use a concordance and trace each of the Greek words to
the equivalent English word in our versions. (3) The simplest method, however, is to make use of an interlinear
version such as has been discussed in Chapter Five. By
comparing the Greek text of the interlinear translation
with the Greek text printed in the commentary and the
Greek words in the text, we can make use of such relatively
difficult works as these with little trouble.

An interlinear would show us that when Alford mentions *hosa,* for example (in the first sentence quoted above),
he is speaking of the word rendered "whatever" in the
NASB. Similarly, *ei tis* is seen to be "if there is anything"

in the NASB. The other words mentioned, if not translated by the author can be determined just as easily, and we can then share in the opinions and conclusions of a great Greek scholar in our studies of the New Testament.

Reconciliation

Suppose, however, that we are interested in a particular word, not a specific passage of the New Testament (the same problem we faced in Chapter Six). Just as before, one method is to use a concordance to find the first occurrence of a particular Greek word in the New Testament, then locate the comments under that passage in the commentary. However, in a work such as *The Expositor's Greek Testament,* this does not always hold true, because the comments on the different New Testament books are written by different scholars, and there is no real continuity between the different expositions. How can we approach the problem in a situation like this?

Step One. Let's take the important word "reconciliation" as an example. By consulting a concordance such as *Strong's* or *Young's,* we find that this English word occurs only three times and is the rendering of two different words. However, a careful study in comparison with modern versions will show that *hilaskomai* (rendered "reconciliation" in Hebrews 2:17) is more correctly "propitiation." The Greek word *katallagē* is actually the word which forms the basis of our English conception of "reconciliation." We can see that this word is found twice in 2 Corinthians 5. Glancing briefly at the entries for "reconcile," we find that *katallassō* (obviously a related word) is rendered "reconcile" six times, and three of these occurrences are in 2 Corinthians 5. The logical step, therefore, is to consult the comments on 2 Corinthians 5, which is actually the great chapter of reconciliation in the New Testament.

Step Two. Using the same procedure as above, we find that the comments on 2 Corinthians 5:18 (the first verse in this chapter containing the words "reconcile" and "reconciliation") are found on page 72, Volume Three. The comments (by the late J. H. Bernard) are as follows:

tou katallaxantos. . . . *who reconciled us, sc.* all mankind, *to Himself through Christ.* The words *katallassō, katallagē* should be studied in all the contexts where they occur. The verb signifies (i.) *to exchange* and (ii.) *to reconcile,* i.e., to re-establish friendly relations between two parties who are estranged, no matter on which side the antagonism exists. Thus in Matthew 5:24 it is the brother who has *given* offense (not the one who has *received* it) that is spoken of as "being reconciled" to the other. And so too St. Paul's usage is to speak of man being reconciled to God. . . .The important point in the present passage is that it is God Himself who is the ultimate Author of this reconciliation (cf. Romans 5:8, 8:31,32 and especially John 3:16). That the reconciliation is "through Christ" is the heart of the Gospel of the Atonement (cf. Romans 3:24, Colossians 1:20, etc.).

A careful study of this passage (2 Corinthians 5), the above quote, and the references he gives will shed much light on the exceedingly important doctrine of reconciliation.

Suggestions for Further Study

For those who have access to these or similar works, the following words and passages are suggested for further study and practice:

1. *Synonyms. chronos* and *kairos:* words for "times" and "seasons"; *deilia, phobos,* and *eulabeia:* words for "fear"; *zēlos* and *phthonos:* words for "envy."

2. *Individual words.* Try some of these great New Testament words: "convert/conversion"; "resurrection"; "propitiation." There are also a number of words which occur only once in the New Testament and which are not covered in many works, but which are often considered in detail in the scholarly works discussed in this chapter. Some of these are: *penichros:* "poor" in Luke 21:2, *egkratēs:* "temperate" in Titus 1:8; *boēthos:* "helper" in Hebrews 13:6.

3. *Passages.* First Timothy 3:2–7 lists the qualifications for an overseer and is very instructive when considered in the Greek New Testament; Hebrews 1:3 tells us more about the nature of Christ.

9

THE GOD-BREATHED BOOK

In the first chapter we dealt with some treasures rescued from the rubbish heaps of Egypt. These were the papyri—everyday documents of New Testament times which have shed immense light on the Greek New Testament. Yet there have been other, and perhaps more valuable, discoveries made in the trash bins of the East.

Codex Sinaiticus

In May 1844 a young German scholar named Konstantin von Tischendorf arrived at Saint Catherine's Monastery, an imposing structure located at the foot of Mount Sinai. His purpose was to search for old manuscripts of the Bible.

The young scholar had recently distinguished himself in the field of New Testament studies by being the first to transcribe the entire text of an important Biblical manuscript. Tischendorf was elated by his success but was convinced that there were older and better manuscripts yet to be found. He tells of what happened after his arrival at Saint Catherine's:

In visiting the library of the monastery . . . I perceived in the middle of the great hall a large and wide basket full of old parchments; and the librarian, who was a man of information, told me that two heaps of papers like these, mouldered by time, had been already committed to the flame. (Ira M. Price, *The Ancestry of Our Engish Bible,* Harper and Brothers).

Tischendorf became so excited over these finds—when he saw them to be ancient Greek manuscripts of the Bible— that the monks at Saint Catherine's became suspicious. They began to suspect that they had something valuable in their possession and hence allowed Tischendorf to take only one-third of the parchments—about forty-three sheets in all.

Tischendorf returned to Germany with these and published them the same year. Some years later, with funds provided for a more extensive search, the scholar returned to the monastery. At first he found nothing. Then, following a month of fruitless searching, he was invited to the cell of the steward of the convent for some refreshment. Tischendorf remarks:

Scarcely had he entered the room, when, resuming our former subject of conversation he said, "And I, too, have read a Septuagint (ancient Greek translation of the Old Testament).". . . And so saying he took down from the corner of the room a bulky kind of volume, wrapped in a red cloth, and laid it before me. I unrolled the cover and discovered, to my great surprise, not only those fragments which fifteen years before I had taken out of the basket, but also other parts of the Old Testament, the New Testament complete, and in addition, the Epistle of Barnabas and part of the Pastor of Hermas (noncanonical books from the early Christian era). Full of joy which this time I had the self-command to conceal from the steward and the rest of the community, I asked, as if in a careless way, for permission to take the manuscript into my sleeping chamber to look over it more at leisure. I knew that I held in my hand the most precious Biblical treasure in existence.

Eventually, though not without difficulty, Tischendorf managed to secure the entire manuscript, which he presented to the Czar of Russia, and in 1862 published the entire text. Later, in 1933, the manuscript was purchased by the British government for one-half million dollars and placed in the British Museum in London.

What was this manuscript? And why all this excitement over an old book? This codex (a codex is a name for a manuscript which was cut and bound in book form as opposed to the older scrolls or rolls) has been named the *Codex Sinaiticus,* from the location at which it was found. It is regarded as one of the two oldest codices of the New Testament in existence. It has been estimated at having been copied out in 340 A.D. The other oldest codex is the *Vaticanus,* dated sometime before 350 A.D.

The only older manuscripts which we have are papyrus fragments. Some of these date from before 200 A.D. and are quite valuable in determining the text of the New Testament. However, they are incomplete in most cases, some fragments containing only a few verses, though others may have whole chapters or even books.

It is not only in age, however, that the *Codex Sinaiticus* is distinguished, but also in preservation. As can be imagined, most of the books and papers of old times were not as fortunate as the Egyptian papyri, which had a dry climate to help preserve them. The *Sinaiticus,* however, is in an excellent state of preservation. This is partially due to the material on which it was written. This codex was at one time quite valuable, even when it was first produced. It was written on some three hundred and forty-six and one-half (346¼) pages of the very best quality of antelope skins (dried and stretched: called vellum). The skins alone would have been worth a small fortune at that time.

Textual Criticism

My wife once confided to me that, previous to our marriage, she had always thought that the "originals" of the Bible (the Hebrew Bible and The Greek New Testament) still existed just as originally written down by the Biblical writers, kept locked and secured in a vast mysterious vault "over there." It may come as a surprise to a number of people to realize that we have no trace of the actual original manuscripts (also called autographs) of the Bible, either Old or New Testaments. What we *do* have are copies—hundreds and thousands of copies!

According to a recent list prepared by textual critics, there are some five thousand copies or manuscripts of the Greek New Testament which survive. Most of these are incomplete. These can be roughly divided as follows: less than a hundred of these are papyrus manuscripts, since the papyrus (being the oldest and written on a lesser quality of writing material) survived the least time, though there were probably a greater number of these originally than of any other kind. In fact, the original manuscripts of the New Testament (such as Paul's letters, for example) were probably written on parchment. Less than three hundred of these five thousand manuscripts are known as majuscles or uncials (because they were printed by hand in all capital letters). These are the codices such as *Sinaiticus* and *Vaticanus*.

Then there are almost three thousand known minuscules: these are also known as cursives and are written in smaller letters or flowing writing. These are generally, but not always, of a more recent date than the uncials.

Finally, there are over two thousand lectionaries. These are manuscripts containing the Scripture lessons to be read publicly in the churches, and copied by hand during the Middle Ages.

These five thousand or so surviving and known manuscripts are all in Greek. This does not include the thousands of manuscripts and fragments which survive in other ancient languages and translations, including Latin, Syriac, Coptic, Armenian, etc. These must all be considered by the textual critic.

You may be wondering, Why are all these manuscripts important? After all, don't they all say the same thing? You may already have noticed in your studies that not only are there differences between versions, but there are also differences between different Greek texts of the New Testament. For example, the Greek text in Marshall's interlinear translation is different in some places from the text in Berry's interlinear version. These differences are usually small and relatively insignificant. They result from the fact that there are differences—also small and usually unimportant from a standpoint of interpretation—in the various Greek manuscripts which survive.

Why aren't all the ancient manuscripts identical? Try copying out even one of the longer books of the New Testament by hand sometime; when you get through you will probably be surprised at the number of errors you have made. These errors are of course innocently made and usually related to spelling, transposition of words, etc. Remember, however, that you are copying from a printed, easily read source, whereas the oldest manuscripts of the Bible were printed by hand, in all capital letters, with no punctuation or spaces between the lines, and copies were made from such manuscripts as these.

Take the following example of the first two lines of Acts 1:1 as written in the *Codex Sinaiticus* (reproduced here, remember, not in handwritten but in printed type):

ΤΟΝΜΕΝΠΡΩΤΟ̄
ΛΟΓΟΝΕΠΟΙΗΣΑ

Now look at the way this would appear as transcribed into English characters with proper punctuation and spacing (note the divided word at the end of line two):

ton men prōton
logon epoiēsa-

Finally, let's look at this passage in English (NASB) written with all capitals, no punctuation or spacing, and you can begin to appreciate the complexities facing the Greek scholar and textual critic (and remember that this is a fairly simple passage compared with many passages in the New Testament):

THEFIRSTACCOUNTICOMPOSEDTHEOPHILUSABOUTALL

These differences between manuscripts help explain some of the differences in readings between various translations of the Bible. For example, when the NASB refers in its footnotes to "Some ancient mss. read . . ." (as, for example, in Romans 8:28,34,35), one of the ancient manuscripts being referred to is the *Sinaiticus*. In some cases, some manuscripts omit verses or readings which others retain, some have one word where others have another, etc. For example, at Luke 23:17 the NASB puts verse 17 in brackets, with a footnote stating, "Many mss. do not contain this v."

Remember, however, that these differences actually affect only a small portion of the text of the New Testament. The late Greek scholar A. T. Robertson concluded that there could be real concern over no more than one thousandth of the text of the Greek Testament. This means that the basic text is 99.9 percent free of significant variations.

Which Greek Testament?

Why so much talk about textual criticism? One reason is because as we learn to use a number of Greek study aids, we will soon encounter this problem. Even the simpler Greek word studies, such as Wuest and Vincent, give alternate readings based on different manuscripts. We will also encounter this many times in modern translations, and there are often questions and discussions about this subject in Bible study or Sunday school classes.

The object of this book, however, is not to deal with textual criticism, but with the Greek Testament itself. For those interested in more information about the subject of textual criticism, a number of works ranging from simple introductions to more complex studies are listed in Appendix C. However, the problem posed is this: which Greek Testament should I use? Just as there are a number of translations, there are also a number of Greek Testaments. The one which agrees with the text from which the King James Version was made is referred to as the Textus Receptus or Received Text. This text is found in Berry's interlinear, for example, and is also the basis for a few modern translations, including Young's *Literal Translation* and Jay Green's *Twentieth-Century King James Version* (see Appendix C). Other Greek Testaments of a former era include Tischendorf's text and the Westcott and Hort text. This latter text influenced the King James revisers (both of the English 1885 and the American 1901 editions) to a great extent. However, these older texts have generally been replaced in modern times by other works, and most modern translations are usually based on one of two texts—the Nestle text or that of the United Bible Societies—or else they use an eclectic text determined by the translators themselves. Among those who have used the Nestle text are Wuest and the NASB. The Today's English Version is based on the United Bible Societies text.

What does all this have to do with the layman or English reader? By checking into the matter of textual criticism, one will find that it is certainly not a simple science. There are a number of factors involved which render it difficult ever to arrive at a definitive text of the New Testament (which, of course, shouldn't at all keep us from *trying* to do so). In recent years there have been a number of controversies regarding the subject of textual criticism and which Greek Testament is the best to use. Unfortunately, many of the arguments on both sides have been facile and naive. It is not generally expected that the average reader will become involved greatly with the subject of textual criticism, but we would warn you here—as previously—not to jump to conclusions in regard to these controversies.

Which Greek Testament should you use? This will depend in part on your own preference for a translation. You will probably choose one which matches the translation you are using, as indicated above.

Can a layman use the Greek New Testament? Yes, certainly, especially if one is making use of an interlinar translation (this is another factor which will influence your choice of a Greek Testament). But is it really necessary to be able to use the Greek New Testament? No, not at all. Neither for the study of vocabulary nor for the consideration of grammar is it essential to be able to use the Greek Testament itself. But many readers will *want* to do so because it is both enjoyable and convenient. It not only helps us in our studies of the New Testament, but it also facilitates the use of some of the study aids which we have already considered.

The tools which we will study in the next two chapters will enable us to use the Greek text itself, easily in the case of an interlinear version and with slightly more difficulty (but still not hard) in the case of a plain Greek Testament.

The Greek New Testament is exactly like our English New Testaments in regard to number and order of books, chapters, etc. (This is in contrast to a Hebrew Bible or Old Testament, which arranges the books of the Old Testament quite differently than in our English versions: the order of books in our English Old Testaments is derived from the Septuagint, the ancient Greek translation of the Hebrew Bible.) In most cases, for example, even the titles of the books are similar enough to English so that the non-Greek reader can readily identify them, as we discovered in the last chapter. Of course, for those who do not wish to use a Greek Testament, all of the grammatical aids which we are about to consider, as well as those aids which we have already discussed, can be used in connection with any English version.

The Grammar of the New Testament

Arriving at a text of the New Testament is only the first step. The next step for the Bible expositor or translator involves vocabulary: determining what the words (which we have decided through textual criticism actually belong in the New Testament) really mean. In the first part of this book we have been concerned with vocabulary or the meanings of individual words.

There is another step, however. This involves grammar

and syntax. Grammar involves the changes which individual words undergo (depending on how they are used),
while syntax concerns how these individual words relate
to each other when used together in phrases, clauses, or
sentences. In the next two chapters we will be looking at
the subject of grammar and syntax. But first let's take a
moment to get an overview of the subject. Just what is
Greek syntax and why is it necessary for us to know anything about it?

It should be pointed out that Greek grammar is an
involved and often complicated discipline when considered in all its facets and ramifications. In a book of this
sort, our purpose is not specifically to deal with Greek
grammar, but with Greek study aids involving grammar.
In order to use these grammatical aids, however, it is
necessary to understand certain basic and simple terms.

First, don't let the word "grammar" frighten you. Those
who have had unfortunate experiences with grammar
in high school or college may be pleasantly surprised to
learn that the study of grammar—at least as applied to
the New Testament—can be both exciting and immensely
rewarding.

Such study is also vitally important, especially to anyone
who interprets or desires to interpret the Bible. Dr. James
Barr mentions the dangers of confining one's approach to
New Testament interpretation exclusively to the lexicons
(word-meaning alone) and suggests that syntax and style
are likely to be more rewarding: "Theological thought of
the type found in the New Testament has its characteristic
linguistic expression not in the word individually but in the
word-combination or sentence" (*The Semantics of Biblical
Language*).

Greek grammar is usually divided into a number of

subjects or sections. In the next two chapters we will consider these sections one at a time. We will cover those topics which will be most helpful and interesting to the layman or English reader and which are necessary to know in order to get the most use from our Greek study tools.

A Word of Caution

In Chapter Twelve the reader is advised of a number of warnings relating to the entire field of Greek study aids, but it would not be amiss to consider a warning here before we begin the study of Greek grammar in particular. Remember that Greek grammar is a vast and complicated field and that the Greek language is highly sophisticated and exact. One of the greatest hindrances in dealing with almost any language is not the rules of grammar but the exceptions to the rules: the irregular words and constructions, etc. To every rule that is illustrated in the following pages there can be found numerous exceptions, which we will not cover here but which do occur in the Greek New Testament. It may well be asked: if the rules and definitions do not always apply, what is the point in studying them? For some important reasons: (1) These definitions apply most of the time. For example, we point out in the next chapter that a Greek aorist tense is usually translated by an English simple past tense. This is not always true, but it is true in probably ninety percent of the cases in the New Testament. It is therefore a valuable rule to know. (2) Most exceptions to these rules have interest primarily for the specialist and often do not affect the primary or essential meaning of a passage.

Generalizations can always be misleading, but they do not have to be. When you are learning to use such aids and encounter a passage that seems to be an exception to the general rules, don't jump to conclusions! Don't try to formulate your own system of Greek grammar or base a new interpretation of a Bible passage on it. Wait until you can obtain more information, consult more reference works and commentaries, speak to a scholar about it, etc.

References to Greek grammar are becoming much more frequent as interest in the original languages of the Bible increases by leaps and bounds. You will find pastors, Sunday school teachers, lessons, commentaries, Bible study guides, etc., referring to the Greek aorist tense, periphrastic constructions, and other similar subjects. This is why it is important to know at least the basics of the terminology and force of Greek grammar. Knowing that a word is an aorist is meaningless unless we know what an aorist is. And knowing that a word is a perfect tense can be misleading if we attempt to equate it with an English perfect.

Remember, however, that the purpose of this book is to help you learn to use Greek study aids, not to make you an expert in New Testament Greek. This will provide a beginning and not a definitive knowledge. It will enable you to begin to use not just translations of the New Testament but the original God-breathed (see 2 Timothy 3:16 in the Greek) Book itself—the Greek New Testament.

10

GRAMMATICAL AIDS

VERBS

In this chapter we will consider grammatical and syntactical aids which have reference to verbs and verb forms. It is in the study of the verb that the beauty and intricate exactness of the Greek language is really displayed. However, there are a few grammatical terms relating to verbs that we need to understand before attempting to use grammatically related study aids. The reason for this is not that the study aids themselves are more difficult to use—most are as simple as the vocabulary aids—but because the terms used to describe Greek verbs are not always equivalent to the corresponding terms in English grammar.

The Greek Verb

First let's look at the basic character of the Greek verb. It is important to realize that the Greek verb is much more complex than the English verb. That is, Greek verbs give us much more information in themselves and do not require as many auxiliary verbs as do English verbs. This is because Greek is a highly inflected language. The basic stems of Greek verbs also change to show gender, number, tense, mood, etc. This is also true to a certain extent in English. For example, "he ran," "she runs," etc. Here the basic verb "to run" is changed to "ran" for a simple past tense, "runs" for a simple present, etc. The changes in Greek verbs are much more numerous and complex, however. A Greek verb can change into as many as five hundred different forms. For example, take the verb *pisteuō*, "I believe." This word changes to *pisteueis* for "you (singular) believe"; to *pisteuei* for "he believes"; to *pisteuomen* for "we believe"; to *pisteusō* for "I will believe," etc.

However, though learning these inflections of Greek verbs is an essential part of the study of Greek grammar for the Greek student, it is not at all necessary for the English reader. For the non-Greek student, the use of aids will help us readily to identify the form of any verb in the New Testament.

But there is one aspect of the Greek verb that is essential for us to know if we are to get any real help from our studies. This is the peculiar character of the Greek tense.

In English, we have the idea that "tense" of a verb relates only to the *time* of the action, and our terms are coined to express this concept. In Greek, however, the primary aspect of tense is not *time* but the *kind or character* of the action—whether in progress, completed, or indefinite (that is, conceived of as a simple event without reference to progress or completion). The late Greek scholar Ernest De Witt Burton remarked: "The chief function of a Greek tense is not to denote time, but progress. This latter function belongs to the tense-forms of all the moods. The former to those of the Indicative only." (*Syntax of Moods and Tenses*).

In view of this fact, many grammarians have felt that the word "tense" is misleading and have attempted to coin other terms, such as the German *aktionsärt*. However, none of these have really become accepted generally in all circles, and we will continue to speak of them as tenses.

It is important to understand the particular function of the different Greek tenses and moods before examining specific study aids. Therefore we will first look at each one briefly and with some clarifying examples before considering the grammatical tools and how to use them.

The Greek verb has seven tenses and four moods. The tenses are the present, imperfect, aorist, future, perfect, pluperfect, and future perfect. The moods are subjunctive, optative, imperative, and indicative. In addition, there are two verbal forms used often in the New Testament which we will consider briefly. These are the participle (strictly speaking, a verbal adjective) and the infinitive (a verbal noun).

Remember, as explained previously, that these definitions of grammatical terms are greatly simplified. For a more detailed discussion, any of the grammars listed in Appendix C can be consulted.

Greek Tenses

1. *Present Tense.* The present tense in Greek denotes action in progress. This is also true in English theoretically, but the English simple present is often equivalent to an imperfect. For example, "he runs to the store" could express that he is at present in the process of running to the store. However, it could express repeated or habitual action—i.e., that he is in the habit of running (rather than walking, driving, etc.) to the store. As can be seen, action in progress is often expressed in English by a present participle, "he is running." Remember, therefore, that a

Greek present may not always be rendered in English by a present, or, if it is, remember that it refers (in most cases) to a simple action presently in progress rather than to habitual action.

Examples in the New Testament of the present tense are numerous: In John 3:5 (NASB): "Truly, truly, I say to you," the verb *legō* (to say) is in the present tense and expresses the fact that "I am saying to you right now, at this very moment."

2. *Imperfect Tense.* The imperfect tense in Greek generally represents action in progress in past time (as the present does in present time) or it refers to repeated or habitual action. Take, for example, *epipraskon kai diemerizon* in Acts 2:45: "they were selling . . . and dividing" their property or possessions. The two imperfects inform us that this action was customary and repeated. It was not just that "they sold . . . and parted" (KJV) on one occasion, but it was the habit of these early Christians of Jerusalem to do so at this time.

3. *Aorist Tense.* One of the most important and most frequently used tenses in the New Testament is the aorist. This verb, though usually rendered by an English past tense, has no real connection with time of action. The time is to be derived from the context. Whereas the present and imperfect tenses have to do with action in progress, the aorist is not concerned with the progress of an action, whether the action is viewed as repeated or completed. Nor is it true that the aorist necessarily refers, as is sometimes affirmed, to a one-time or once-for-all action. Burton remarks that "the aorist . . . is most frequently used to express a past event viewed in its entirety, simply as an event or a single fact. It has no reference to the progress of the event, or to any existing result of it." (*Syntax*).

Examples are frequent, particularly in narratives:

These things Jesus *spoke* (John 17:4 NASB).
I *glorified* Thee on the earth (John 17:4 NASB).
I *manifested* Thy name (John 17:6 NASB).

However, the aorist is not always to be viewed as a past tense or an event in past time. As the preface to the NASB New Testament points out: "Not all aorists have been rendered as English pasts ('He did'), for some of them are clearly to be rendered as English perfects ('He has done'), or even as past perfects ('He had done'), judging from the context in which they occur."

Remembering these exceptions, it is found in ninety percent of the cases that a simple aorist can be rendered by an English past.

In using grammatical works, we will find references to "first aorist" and "second aorist" or "aorist one" and "aorist two." These distinctions, however, refer to the inflections or conjugations of the verbs (those in class two being formed differently from those in class one) and *not* to their grammatical meanings. These differentiations can therefore be safely ignored by the English reader.

4. *Future Tense.* This tense, as in English, refers to an action which will take place in the future (in relation to the speaker or to the context) and is more tense-or time-related than the previous tenses. The future tense does not distinguish between action in progress or action as a simple event. It simply determines that it is either to take place or begin to take place at some time *after* the moment of speaking, See, for example:

You *shall receive* power (Acts 1:8 NASB).
You *shall be* My witnesses (Acts 1:8 NASB).

This Jesus . . . *will come* (Acts 1:11 NASB)

5. *Perfect Tense.* This is another important and often misunderstood tense. One reason it is often misinterpreted is simply because this tense, more than the others, differs from that which is called "perfect" in English. Grammarians Dana and Mantey define the perfect as "the tense of complete action. Its basal significance is the progress of an act or state to a point of culmination and the existence of its finished results. That is, it views action as a finished product" (*A Manual Grammar of the Greek New Testament*).

The perfect, therefore, has a double emphasis: it refers to a present *state* resulting from past *action.* An example is found in John 1:34:

And I *have seen* and *have borne witness* that this is the Son of God" (NASB).

J. Harold Greenlee illustrates the double force of the perfect by rendering it:

And I am in a condition resulting from having seen, and I have borne an abiding testimony (*A Concise Exegetical Grammar of New Testament Greek,* Eerdmans).

It is sometimes asserted that the result in the perfect tense is permanent, but while this is sometimes true it is not always so. The basic characteristic of the perfect is that *at the time of speaking* the result still stands. For example, Luke 24:46 reads:

Thus it is written, that the Christ should suffer and rise again from the dead the third day (NASB).

"Thus it is written" is "It *stands* written"; i.e., "it has been written down (at some point in the past) and is presently on record." With God's Word, as here, the result may be viewed as permanent (see Isaiah 40:8), but this is derived from the context or related data and not from the tense itself.

Burton cautions, however, that "it is important to observe that the term "complete" or "completed" as a grammatical term does not mean *ended,* but *accomplished,* i.e., brought to its appropriate result, which result remains at the time denoted by the verb" (*Syntax*).

Burton also points out the essential difference between the aorist and the perfect, both of which have to do with past time. "The aorist and the perfect both involve reference to a past event, the perfect affirming the existence of the result of the event, and the aorist affirming the event itself, without either affirming or denying the existence of the results " (*Syntax*).

Remember that the aorist is concerned simply with the event and not with any results thereof, though there may *be* results. The perfect, on the other hand, is concerned with the results rather than with the event itself, the event being viewed as a necessary prerequisite for the present results.

6. *Pluperfect Tense.* The pluperfect also has a double emphasis: the past state resulting from previous action. It is often rendered by an English past perfect. An example is found in Luke 8:2: "Mary who was called Magdalene, from whom seven demons *had gone out*" (NASB); i.e., the past act was not only begun but *completed* at some point in the past.

William LaSor remarks that "The pluperfect tense, like the perfect, conveys the idea of existing state as a result of completed action. It differs from the perfect only in this: its point of view is in the past" (*Handbook of New Testament Greek*).

7. *Future Perfect Tense.* According to most grammarians, the simple future perfect does not exist in the New Testament (though it was used commonly in secular and classical Greek). About four times, however, a periphrastic future perfect occurs: in Matthew 16:19; 18:18; Luke 12:52; and Hebrews 2:13.

The well-known passage from Matthew 16:19 will suffice as an example of this rare situation. First we need to explain the term "periphrastic." This word comes from two Greek words: *peri,* meaning "around," and *phrazō,* meaning "to declare." It refers to a roundabout expression or way of saying something. For example, instead of using a simple verb such as *edidaske* (imperfect: "he was teaching"), a writer might choose to use an auxiliary verb followed by a participle, such as *ēn didaskōn* ("he was teaching").

In Matthew 16:19 ("Whatever you shall bind on earth *shall be bound* in heaven," NASB) we have a construction which equals a future perfect in force but is not a single verb in Greek, but two verbs: a simple future ("shall be") followed by a perfect passive participle (literally "having been bound"). The entire phrase would therefore read: "Whatever you shall bind on earth shall be having been bound in heaven." J. B. Phillips, in one of the rare notes in his popular translation, remarks on this passage:

> There is a very curious Greek construction here. Can anyone explain why the simple future passive is not used? It seems to me that . . . the force of these sayings is that Jesus' true disciples will be so led by the Spirit that they will be following the heavenly pattern. In other words what they "forbid" or "permit" on earth will be consonant with the Divine rule. There is no ground for supposing that celestial endorsement automatically follows human action, however exalted.

Greek Moods and Voices

In addition to tense, the Greek verb also has mood and voice.

1. *The indicative mood* is "primarily the mood of the unqualified assertion or simple question of fact" (Burton, *Syntax*). This is the most common and simple of the moods. It is used in simple narrative speech, declarative sentences, simple questions, etc. There are numerous examples. The first in the New Testament is "Abraham *begat* Isaac" (Matthew 1:2 KJV).

2. *The subjunctive mood* expresses wish, intention, possibility, or probability. It is referred to as the mood of "contingency" and is often used with an "if," "might," or other qualifying word. An example is found in Matthew 2:22: "that what was spoken through the prophets *might be fulfilled*" (NASB). The subjunctive is shown here through the use of the word "might," indicating that the fulfillment of this particular prophecy was contingent upon these events having taken place which had just occurred.

3. *The imperative mood* is, as in English, the mood of command. It is used also in exhortations and has some unusual uses which we will consider in later examples. Its simple use is seen in Matthew 2:8: "And he [Herod] sent them to Bethlehem, and said, 'Go and *make careful search* for the Child; and when you have found Him, *report* to me'" (NASB).

4. *The optative mood* occurs only rarely in the New Testament. It is the mood of "wishing," and almost all examples of this mood in the New Testament are drawn from prayers. An example is found in 1 Peter 1:2: "*May* grace and peace be yours *in fullest measure* [literally, may it be multiplied]" (NASB).

In regard to *voice,* the Greek verb may either be active, passive, or middle. The first two voices function exactly as in English. The active voice shows the subject as the *performer* of the action ("Abraham *begat* Isaac," Matthew 1:2 KJV), while the passive shows the subject as the *recipient* of the action ("Mary, by whom *was born* Jesus" Matthew 1:16 NASB).

The middle voice, however, may require a brief explanation. It has been remarked that the middle voice is "one of the most distinctive and peculiar phenomena of the Greek language. It is impossible to describe it, adequately or accurately, in terms of English idiom, for English knows no approximate parallel. We can never hope to express exactly the Greek middle voice by an English translation, but must seek to acclimate ourselves to its mental atmosphere, and feel its force, though we cannot express it precisely" (Dana and Mantey, *Manual Grammar*).

The middle voice is, in some ways, a combination of the active and the passive. Dana and Mantey remark "the middle voice is that use of the verb which describes the subject as *participating in the results of the action.* Thus *bouleuō* means "I counsel," but *bouleuomai* means "I take counsel," the subject acting with a view to participation in the outcome" (*Manual Grammar*).

A good example of the use of the middle voice is found in Matthew 27:5: "And he [Judas] went away and *hanged himself*" (NASB).

However, it should be pointed out that many, if not most, of the "middles" found in the New Testament are actually deponent. Benjamin Chapman explains that "A verb is said to be *deponent* (misplaced) if it has an active meaning in context but a middle or passive form" (*A Card Guide to New Testament Exegesis II*). The Bible student must

be aware of this fact and should consult a reputable gram·
mar (such as those listed in Appendix C) when in doubt as
to the role of a particular middle or passive verb in a
particular context.

Related Verbal Forms

There are also two forms which are closely associated
with verbs: the infinitive and the participle.

1. *The infinitive* is sometimes classified as a mood and
listed in lieu of the mood when parsed (see below), but it
is actually a verbal noun: a word with some characteristics
of the verb and some of the noun. The function of the
infinitive in Greek is quite similar to its function in English.
An example of the infinitive functioning as a verb is found
in Matthew 2:2:

"For we . . . have come *to worship* Him" (NASB).

An example of its use as a noun is found in Philippians
1:21:

"To live is Christ, and *to die* is gain" (NASB).

2. *The participle* "is a verbal adjective, sharing in part the
characteristics of both the verb and the adjective" (Burton,
Syntax). It describes its subject as a doer or performer of
the action indicated by the verb. The participle always has
a tense, and can have any of the tenses indicated above.
An example of a present participle is found in Matthew
1:23:

"Immanuel, which *translated* means, "God With Us" (NASB).

An example of the aorist participle is found in Matthew
1:24:

"And Joseph arose [literally, *having risen,* or *having been aroused*] from his sleep, and did as the angel of the Lord commanded him (NASB).

As can be seen, the participle often describes an action *in progress.* However, it takes its character from the tense employed. It is often used, too, with another—primary—verb, as in the second example above. In this case the participle describes action which is simultaneous with or previous to the primary verb or verbs. The participle also functions adjectivally, examples of which will be seen later on.

Grammatical Study Aids

The tools which will be of help to us in understanding the grammar of the New Testament can be divided into several classes.

1. The first of these includes standard grammars. We will not consider the use of these here (other than to quote from them occasionally, as above) since such works are simply textbooks and reference books and can be used in exactly the same manner as any other language textbook. Some grammars are simple and intended for the beginning Greek student; others are comprehensive and designed for the use of the Greek scholar. A large list of such works is shown in Appendix C.

2. The second group includes purely grammatical tools. The most useful works in this class are *An Analytical Greek Lexicon* and Nathan Han's *Parsing Guide to the Greek New Testament.* The latter work considers verbs and verb forms only; the former work lists every word in the Greek New Testament, analyzes the word grammatically (referred to as "parsing"), then indicates the basic or dictionary form.

This work also serves as a standard lexicon in that definitions are supplied under the basic form of the words.

3. The third group includes works which provide information on both vocabulary and grammar. Representative works are *A Grammatical Analysis of the Greek New Testament,* by Max Zerwick and Mary Grosvenor; *A Linguistic Key to the Greek New Testament,* by Fritz Rienecker; and *The Analytical Greek New Testament,* by T. and B. Freiberg.

4. The fourth group includes works which are primarily concerned with vocabulary (contrast the above group) but which also contain a certain amount of grammatical information. In this category we place the various English and Greek word studies which we have previously considered (Wuest, Vincent, Alford, etc.).

5. The fifth category deals with some works which we have also examined previously: translations and study Bibles. Among the most helpful here are the literal translations and the *Newberry Reference Bible.*

We will consider the use of at least one work from each main category (with the exception of the first) and see how each can be used to the fullest advantage.

The World's Greatest Sermon

For our examples we will look at some concrete practical teaching from the world's greatest sermon: Matthew 5—7. There have probably been more works written and sermons preached on these three chapters than on any comparable section of Scripture. Yet, despite their great familiarity, there is always something new to learn from this Sermon on the Mount.

Please note that we will be concerned primarily with grammar, not vocabulary, in these examples. However, a vocabulary study using the aids already introduced, will also be most rewarding for the reader who pursues it.

1. *Translations and Study Bibles* (Matthew 5:1-2). We will begin with the simplest aids first. Note that these two verses are an introduction to the discourse proper, but are full of interest from a grammatical point of view. It is not readily apparent from most versions, but there are three basic sentences here, arranged grammatically as parallels. First let's look at the NASB version, arranged to illustrate this parallelism and the force of the clauses:

(And when He saw the multitudes), He went up on the mountain;
(and after He sat down), His disciples came to Him.
(And opening His mouth) He began to teach them,
saying. . . .

To understand the reason for this arrangement, let's look at the *Newberry Reference Bible* to see what the words as employed here are grammatically. This reference Bible is quite valuable for the English reader. By using a system of logical symbols (e.g., a *dot* for the aorist, a *vertical line* for the present, etc.), Newberry points out the tense of every verb in the Bible. However, these symbols do not include information on moods, voice, etc. Therefore we will find it helpful to make use of other aids as well. But for the non-Greek reader, this is one of the simplest grammatical aids, since it does not involve dealing with Greek words at all. Even here, however, it is necessary to understand the crucial distinctions between Greek and English tenses if we are to understand correctly and make full use of the grammatical information provided.

We note in this passage that there are two verbs in each sentence (excluding the final "saying"). In each sentence the first verb is an aorist participle. We might render these uniformly as "having seen," "having set down," and "having opened" in order to illustrate the parallelism.

By comparing these verses in Young's *Literal Translation,* we see how helpful such a work can be in regard to grammar. Young renders all three participles consistently and thereby plainly exhibits the parallel nature and force of the different clauses:

And having seen the multitudes, He went up to the mount, and He having sat down, His disciples came to Him, and having opened His mouth, He was teaching them, saying. . . .

Remember that participles are descriptive verbs and are often subordinate to the primary verbs. In this case, by simply skipping the participles and following the phrases with the primary verbs, we can connect the action: "He went up on the mountain. . . . His disciples came to Him. . . . He began to teach them" (NASB). The three participial clauses are subordinate and descriptive of the action of the main verbs in each case. This is brought out in the NASB by the use of "when," "after," and "opening" in the three dependent clauses. The "when" and "after" are not actually found in the Greek but are used to express the proper force of the Greek participle in an idiomatic English manner.

The second verb in each sentence is a simple aorist in the first two cases, but an imperfect in the third instance. This can be seen easily through Newberry's symbols and is perceptible in the NASB by the use of a simple past in the first two instances and the use of *began* in italics in the third. The NASB has an explanatory note in the preface: "A careful distinction has been made in the treatment of the Greek aorist tense (usually translated as the English past, 'He did') and the Greek imperfect tense (rendered either as English past progressive, 'He was doing'; or, if inceptive, 'He *began* to do' or 'He started to do'); or also if customary past, 'He used to do.' 'Began' is italicized if it renders an imperfect tense, in order to distinguish it from the Greek verb for 'begin.' "

The beauty and exactness of the Greek language can already be seen. The first two situations are aorists: simple events without respect to progress or completion, where the time is indicated by the context. But the word "taught" is imperfect, showing progressive action (rather than a static event) in the past time, as the context clearly shows. Here we obviously have inceptive action: "He *began* to teach them. . . ."

Before leaving this class of study aids, let's notice a different use of the participle. In Matthew 5:4 we have, "Blessed are those who mourn, for they shall be comforted" (NASB). In 5:6 we have, "Blessed are those who hunger and thirst for righteousness, for they shall be satisfied" (NASB). By consulting Newberry's symbols, we see that the verbs used in the first part of each sentence are participles. Here we find the participle used adjectivally (as a descriptive word) and as the subject of the sentence.

The Greek text actually reads, in verse 4: "*makarioi hoi penthountes*" ("Blessed the mourning [ones]" or "the mourners"), and in verse 6: "*makarioi hoi peinōntes kai dipsōntes*" ("Blessed the hungering [ones] and thirsting [ones]" or "hungerers and thirsters"). This is quite awkward in English, but it is important for us to see that Christ is here describing an attitude, not just a one-time act. The present tense (showing progress) coupled with the participle (showing characteristic) informs us that Christ is referring to those whose attitude of life is to "mourn" and to "hunger and thirst after righteousness," and not simply to those who may do so on one occasion.

2. *English and Greek Word Studies* (Matthew 5:23-25). In these verses Christ presents some important teaching on forgiveness. In verse 24 He remarks:

First be reconciled to your brother, and then come and present your offering (NASB).

By consulting A.T. Robertson's *Word Pictures* (the procedure for using this and similar work has already been discussed in Chapter Six) on this verse, we find that he analyzes the verb "be reconciled" and informs us that it is a "second aorist passive imperative. Get reconciled (ingressive aorist, take the iniative)." The use of the imperative mood informs us that this is a command or exhortation. Christ does not simply suggest that "it would be nice if you would first be reconciled," but He lays it down as an absolute necessity before presenting your offering. The aorist shows us that we are here concerned with a simple event regardless of any results or effects which might precede or arise from the event. Being reconciled *now* is the important thing, though of course we may have to be reconciled later on, even again and again (see Matthew 18:21-22).

In verse 25, "Make friends quickly with your opponent" (NASB), Robertson informs us that the verb "make friends" is a present periphrastic active imperative (*isthi eunoōn*). This combination is classified as periphrastic because it uses the word "to be" (literally "be agreeing with your opponent") in a present active imperative construction along with the verb "to agree" in a present active participle form. Here the present tense views the action as progressive rather than as a single event in contrast to the previous verse. The participle again shows characteristic action on our parts: we are to be those who customarily "make friends" with our opponents rather than those who continue to hold grudges or stubbornly refuse to "make up."

3. *Grammar and Vocabulary Tools* (Matthew 5:38-42). Jesus here deals with our relations to other people, including those who may be our adversaries or who may use us wrongfully. For this example, let's use Zerwick and Grosvenor's *Grammatical Analysis of the Greek New Testament*. This work (like Rienecker's *Linguistic Key*) is arranged according to the books of the New Testament. The significant words of each verse are analyzed briefly, according to word meaning, basic word form, and grammatical information.

Let's turn to the comments on Matthew 5:38-42. We see that the word "resist" ("Do not resist him who is evil," NASB) is aorist infinitive, *antistēnai*. The aorist views this as a simple event without regard to results or effects. Christ is here conceiving of a specific situation, though He does not thereby deny that this is to be an attitude as well. The infinitive could be rendered like this: "But I say to you not *to resist* the evil."

In verse 40 ("and if anyone wants to sue you," NASB), this work informs us that we have a participle (literally "is wanting") followed by another aorist infinitive ("to sue"). In verse 41 we have an example of the future tense:

Whoever *shall force* you to go one mile, go with him two (NASB).

In verse 42 we have an example of the middle voice:

Do not turn away from him who wants *to borrow* from you (NASB).

This work informs us that "to borrow" (*danisasthai*) is aorist infinitive middle in construction. The aorist refers to the act of borrowing as a simple event. The infinitive illustrates the characteristics of the word as a noun in this sentence. The use of the middle voice shows us that the act of borrowing is twofold: the subject (the one wishing to borrow) participates in the result of the action (receiving the money) by *asking* to borrow. There is therefore action on *both* sides: one asking for money (or other items), the other lending to him.

4. *Analytical Guides and Lexicons* (Matthew 6:9-13). As interesting and helpful as these previous works are, the reader who has advanced to this point will find the most comprehensive information and help supplied by the works in this category. The student who uses these tools will be able to work directly from the Greek text itself, without having to bother with concordances, or other tools for determining the meanings of the Greek words in question. (Of course, the student who wishes to use a concordance or similar tool instead of working from the Greek Testament can do so. After a little practice, however, using the Greek text itself actually takes less time and energy than any other method.)

For our example, we will use an interesting and well-known passage: the "model prayer" taught by Christ. The handiest method, you will recall, for the English reader in approaching a passage of this sort is to use an interlinear version. For example, verse 9 reads in Marshall's Interlinear like this:

οὕτως	οὖν		προσεύχεσθε	ὑμεῖς·	
Thus	therefore		pray		ye:
Πάτερ	ἡμῶν	ὁ		ἐν	τοῖς οὐρανοῖς·
Father	of us	the (one)		in	the heavens:

Ἁγιασθήτω   τὸ   ὄνομά   σου·
Let it be hallowed   the   name   of thee.

Here, of course, we are primarily interested in the verbs. There are two in this verse: "pray" and "let it be hallowed." For this example let's use Nathan Han's *Parsing Guide*. This work is arranged verse-by-verse according to the books of the New Testament. It is a simple matter for the English reader to turn to the section on Matthew 6:9. Here we find the following arrangement:

προσευχεσθε   2 p. pl. pres. mid. ind. (*or imper.*) προσευχομαι
ἁγιασθητω   3 p. sing. 1 aor. pass. imper. ἁγιαζω

Note the format: Han lists the Greek verb in exactly the same form in which it occurs in the Greek Testament, then parses the verb (shows the complete analysis), then indicates the basic or dictionary form so that we can locate the word in a standard lexicon.

The advantage to such works as this is that the author parses the words completely, rather than just giving the information which he considers pertinent.

Here it is a simple matter to compare *proseuchesthe* with the same word in the Greek text above to see that this refers to the word "pray." This verb is listed as second person plural (that is, "you [plural] pray") and present middle. The present illustrates the progressive nature of the verb while the middle here is actually deponent, so that the force of the verb is the same as an active. Note that the word may be either indicative or imperative; in this case, the imperative seems to fit the context better in view of Christ's instruction as exhortation.

The second verb is *hagiasthētō*. This is third person singular ("He"—i.e., our Father) and aorist passive imperative. The passive tells us why Marshall has rendered this as "let it be hallowed" instead of simply "hallowed." The passive voice illustrates the subject as receiving the action rather than performing it. The aorist tense may refer to a definite event at a particular moment in time, though Zerwick and Grosvenor remark: "The aorist [is] customary in prayers and does not necessarily carry eschatological implications" (*Analysis*).

The interesting thing to notice about this verb is that it is in the imperative mood. By using the *Parsing Guide* and an interlinear Greek Testament, we notice that almost all of the verbs in this prayer are in the imperative mood. Yet we have remarked previously that the optative mood is the mood of "wishing and praying." Why, then, are imperatives used in this section?

First let's look at the remainder of this prayer in the NASB, with the force of the verbs pointed out for convenience:

Thy kingdom come (aorist active imperative). Thy will be done (aorist passive imperative), on earth as it is in heaven.

Give (aorist active imperative) us this day our daily bread. And forgive (aorist active imperative) us our debts, as we also have forgiven (aorist active indicative) our debtors. And do not lead (aorist active subjunctive) us into temptation, but deliver (aorist middle imperative) us from evil.

Note the use of the imperative everywhere except in two instances. Instance one: the simple statement of fact in verse 12: "we forgave our debtors." (We see in passing that here is a case where the aorist can legitimately be rendered as a perfect: "have forgiven." This is derived from the context, however, rather than from grammatical reasons. It is obvious that we would not only have to forgive others, but remain in a condition of having forgiven them. To forgive them one moment and then continue to hold a grudge would do little good. Grammatically, however, the emphasis is on the *act* of forgiving, not the results.) Instance two: the subjunctive in verse 13, which could be rendered, "And mayest Thou not lead us to temptation" (*Young's Literal Translation*). This use of the subjunctive (referred to as hortatory subjunctive) is common in negative prohibitions.

Why, though, the use of imperatives? Are we giving God commands? Is it right for us to simply say, "Give us" instead of "Please give us"?

Dr. Eugene A. Nida has an enlightening comment on this in *God's Word in Man's Language*:

For the ancient philosopher and priest of esoteric cults, steeped in the tradition of classical Greek, the grammatical forms of the Lord's Prayer would seem almost rude. One does not find the optative forms of polite petition so characteristic of elaborate requests made to earthly and heavenly potentates. Rather than employing such august forms, the Christians made their requests to God in what seem to be blunt imperatives. This does not mean that Christians lacked respect for their heavenly Father, but it does mean that they were consistent with a new understanding of Him. In the tens of thousands of papyri fragments which have been rescued from the rubbish heaps of the ancient Greek world, one finds the imperative forms used constantly between members of a family. When the Christian addressed God as "Father," it was perfectly natural therefore for him to talk to Him as intimately as they would to their own father.

What insight this throws on prayer! One of the greatest blessings of Christianity is the fact that we have access to the Father through Christ (Ephesians 2:18)! We know from reading the book of Esther, for example, that to enter the presence of an eastern ruler unbidden or uninvited could easily mean death. We find this typified in the *Yom Kippur,* the Day of Atonement in the Old Testament. Only the high priest could enter the holy of holies, and this only on that one special day. Any mistake on his part in the specified ritual (whether through ignorance or design) could easily have meant death. Yet today we have access "by a new and living way which He inaugurated for us through the veil, that is, His flesh" (Hebrews 10:20 NASB), and we are bidden to:

Draw near with confidence to the throne of grace, that we may receive mercy and may find grace to help in time of need" (Hebrews 4:16 NASB).

Yet many of us rarely or never make use of this wonderful privilege of being able to approach God as Father through the perfection and excellence of Christ Himself.

This also throws light on Christ's injunctions regarding prayer—not to pray as the hypocrites or as the Gentiles (Matthew 6:5,7 NASB). We are to make our requests known simply, surely, and confidently—always with the respect due to God, but realizing our acceptance "in the beloved" (Ephesians 1:6 KJV) and with a sense of our need and utter dependence. Should we make long, formal prayers, with no sincerity in them? Would we try to fool our earthly fathers with puffed-up discourse or vain talking?

In Matthew 6:33 we read one of the most familiar but perhaps most-misunderstood verses in the New Testament: "But seek first His kingdom and His righteousness; and all these things shall be added to you" (NASB).

By using Han's *Parsing Guide* and locating this verse, we find that "seek" is a present imperative, not an aorist. This verse does not refer simply to salvation or a once-for-all seeking for salvation. Rather it refers to our day-by-day action of seeking to put God and His kingdom first in our lives. The verse is teaching us perspective, not salvation. This should be our characteristic attitude: be in a state of seeking His kingdom first. It is important that we realize that once we have received Christ into our hearts and lives, it is not the *end* of the Christian life, but just the *beginning.*

Another good example of the importance of distinguishing between the present and the aorist is found in Matthew 7:1: "Do not judge lest you be judged" (NASB). Here "judge" is present active imperative, while "judged" is aorist passive subjunctive. The present imperative used with the negative particle (*mē* = not) tells us that we are to stop doing something already engaged in. It is a command, a prohibition: "Stop judging others." The present views it as a progressive rather than as a one-time action. We might show this as "Stop continually judging others." The reason Christ gives for this is that we may find ourselves judged by God (at a particular point in time) by the same standards which we use on others. We should show mercy and grace when dealing with others because this is how God has dealt with us and is certainly how we wish Him to deal with us in the future.

Matthew 7:13-14 is another one of those passages which have been preached on and expounded thousands of times, yet which are so pregnant with meaning that we can never exhaust them completely. "Enter by the narrow gate; for the gate is wide and the way is broad that leads to destruction, and many are those who enter by it. For the gate is small and the way is narrow that leads to life, and few are those who find it" (NASB).

This passage contains many interesting features, but the most instructive from a grammatical viewpoint is found in verse 14: "The way is *narrow* that leads to life." Notice that this word "narrow" is rendered as an adjective in most versions. Yet by consulting an interlinear version we see that the Greek word rendered "narrow" is actually a verb: *tethlimmenē*. To examine this verb, let's use the *Analytical Greek Lexicon.* This work is arranged differently from Han's *Parsing Guide.* First of all, it includes *every* word in the Greek Testament, not just verbs and verb forms. Secondly, it lists these words alphabetically rather than verse-by-verse. In other words, to find any particular Greek word, you sim-ply take the Greek form of the word as it *actually occurs* in the Greek Testament and locate it in exactly the same manner as with the standard lexicons which we considered in Chapter Seven.

For example, let's take this word *tethlimmenē.* (1) Note the first letter, "tau," and remember to distinguish be-tween "tau" and "theta" ("th"), which also appears in this word. (2) Also remember to differentiate between "epsi-lon" ("e") and "eta" ("ē"), both of which also occur in this word.

Locating the word, we find the following entry (of course, the Greek words are presented in Greek characters in the lexicon itself):

tethlimmenē, nom. sing. fem. part. perf. pass. *thlibō*

This analysis tells us that the word we find here in Matthew 7:14 is a perfect passive participle in construction. The perfect refers to action *completed* in past time, but with continuing results in the present. The passive voice indi-cates that the subject ("the way") is the recipient of the action. The participle shows progressive and characteristic action (in the past time when used here with a perfect). A literal translation, therefore, would read: "The way [is] *having been narrowed* that leads to life." This tells us that "the way" leading to life has been narrowed (by some outside agency) at some time in the past, with the result that it is still in a state of narrowness at the present time. We learn from studying other passages in the New Testament what this "way" actually is: Jesus Christ Himself (see John 14:6).

Suggestions for Further Study

Using any of the aids listed in this chapter, and remembering the significant differences between English and Greek verbs, look at the verbs in these other passages of this great discourse and see how much light is shed on Christ's teaching by carefully distinguishing between different tenses, moods, and voices.

1. The cure for worry: Matthew 6:25-32.
2. Pearls before swine: Matthew 7:6.
3. Making request to God: Matthew 7:7-12.
4. The two builders: Matthew 7:24-27.
5. The epilogue: Matthew 7:28-29 (compare these two verses with the introduction to the discourse: Matthew 5:1-2).

11

GRAMMATICAL AIDS

NOUNS AND MISCELLANEOUS FORMS

In this chapter we will deal with some miscellaneous grammatical forms which are necessary for us to understand if we are to get the utmost benefit out of Greek study aids.

We are concerned with definitions of terms only as they apply to such aids and will be helpful in our use of such aids—not as a course in New Testament Greek. Here we will encounter many terms found frequently in grammatical tools which can be confusing or even misleading if not properly understood.

The Noun

First we will look at nouns, the proper complement of verbs. We will find that the study of nouns is not quite as involved as the study of verbs, but nouns can still be quite revealing in our study of the New Testament.

Nouns are parsed according to gender, number, and case. In English, we are not usually concerned with gender. However, many of the world's major languages classify all nouns as either masculine, feminine, or neuter. This classification must be learned because it is not always obviously logical from our point of view. For example, though man is of course masculine in New Testament Greek, word, world, and death are also masculine.

Similarly, woman is feminine and so are faith, hope, and love.

Some common neuter nouns are spirit, name, and baptism.

Number refers to whether a word is singular or plural. Classical Greek also contains a *dual* form (as does Biblical Hebrew), but this does not occur in New Testament Greek and can be safely ignored by the non-Greek reader.

Case deals with the way a noun is used in a sentence. Dana and Mantey remark: "As used in the expression of a thought, the noun may bear various relations to the rest of the sentence. It may be the subject proper, or it may qualify the subject, or it may function in various ways in the predicate. This variety in the fundamental relations of the noun we call *case*" (*Manual Grammar*).

Benjamin Chapman points out that "subject-object relationships are shown [in Greek] by case, not by word order as in English. For example, in 'The man ate the fish,' which of the two nouns ate the other is shown in Greek by the nominative case form of 'man,' rather than by which comes first in the sentence" (*A Card Guide to New Testament Greek*).

J. Harold Greenlee gives three examples to illustrate why the study of gender, number, and case is of such importance to the Bible student, expositor, or translator. In regard to *case,* he points out that "the agreement of *poimena* ('Shepherd') with *Iēsoun* ('Jesus') and not with *Theos* ('God') in Hebrews 13:20 shows that it is 'Jesus,' not 'God,' who is 'the great shepherd of the sheep.' "

In regard to *gender,* he illustrates with Ephesians 2:8:

For by grace you have been saved through faith; and that not of yourselves, it is the gift of God" (NASB).

He remarks that "*touto* ('that') agrees in gender with neither 'grace' nor 'faith'; it is neuter and means 'this whole condition,' not 'this faith' nor 'this grace.' "

Dealing with *number,* he gives as an example Hebrews 12:14:

Follow peace with all men, and holiness, without which no man shall see the Lord (KJV).

He points out that "both number and gender are involved: *hou,* 'which,' is singular, and therefore cannot refer to *both* 'peace' and 'holiness' . . . but it does agree in gender with 'holiness,' indicating 'apart from holiness no one shall see the Lord' " (*Concise Exegetical Grammar*).

The matter of gender and number requires no further clarification, but the Greek cases are not always exactly equivalent to English cases by the same name, and we will look at them in a little more detail.

Greek is generally and simply recognized to have four primary cases: nominative, genitive, accusative, and dative (the last two correspond to the English objective case). Many grammarians recognize a total of eight cases. These are determined by function, however, and not by inflections of the Greek words. For all ordinary purposes, these four cases will suffice in our consideration of the Greek Testament.

1. *The nominative case* is used when the noun is the subject of the sentence and is the one who performs the action if an active verb is used. For example, "the man walks": "man" is here in the nominative case in English. There are

many examples of the nominative case in the New Testament: "Jesus, finding a young donkey, sat on it" (John
12:14 NASB) is a familiar instance. Here "Jesus" is the
subject of the sentence and is in the nominative case.

2. *The genitive case* shows possession in general. We say,
"the man's book," which indicates that the book is owned
or possessed by the man. However, the genitive case can
be used to indicate a variety of relationships other than
simply possession, and it is in fact one of the most interesting and complex of the Greek cases. Grammarians identify, for example, some fourteen or more different uses of
the genitive, including the following.

The genitive of possession is illustrated in Luke 5:3: "And He
got into one of the boats, which was *Simon's*" (NASB)—i.e.,
Simon's boat.

The genitive of relationship indicates a specific relationship
which exists between two nouns even though the relationship itself may not be spelled out. For example, Acts 13:22
reads: "David the [son] of Jesse" where "son" is omitted
in the Greek text.

The genitive of apposition is used when two words stand
side by side, one further defining the other. For example,
"the temple of His body" (John 2:21)—i.e., "the temple
[which is] His body"; or, "the sign of circumcision" (Romans 4:11)—i.e., "the sign [which is] circumcision."

The genitive of description is used when one noun describes
another. It is often rendered by an adjective in English.
For example, "children of disobedience" (Ephesians 2:2)
—i.e., "disobedient children," children characterized by
disobedience.

Other genitives include the subjective genitive, the objective genitive, the genitive of source, and others. A complete list can be found in any major grammar.

In some cases it is not possible to define exactly the particular force of the genitive case. For example, in 2 Corinthians 5:14 Paul speaks of the fact that "the love of Christ controls us" (NASB). Here the "love of Christ" may refer either to the love Christ bears to us or to the love which we have for Christ. Either case is true, of course, but it cannot be definitely determined from purely grammatical considerations which meaning is intended here.

3. *The accusative case.* Both the accusative and dative cases are cases of object, the former referring to the direct object and the latter to the indirect object. An example of the accusative is found in Matthew 1:2: "Abraham begat *Isaac*" (KJV). Instances of its use are numerous in the New Testament:

> But as many as received Him, to them He gave *the right* to become children of God (John 1:12 NASB).

4. *The dative case,* referring to the indirect object, is found in Matthew 18:26, for example: "I will give you all things." This sentence has both a direct and an indirect object: "I will give all things [direct object] to you [indirect object]." Here *soi* is the dative second person singular form of the pronoun *su* ("you").

There are many other uses and classifications for all four of the cases, but these simple definitions will be most helpful in our studies of the Greek New Testament by means of Greek study aids.

The Pronoun

Closely related to the noun is the pronoun. Dana and Mantey remark on the development and use of the pronoun: "The object before consciousness may be referred to frequently in the same context. To avoid the monotony of repetition the processes of linguistic development have produced the *pronoun*" (*Manual Grammar*).

The importance of the pronoun is seen when we realize that Greek, due to its inflections, does not need to use a pronoun, as English does. For example, in "I will give" above, the pronoun "I" does not actually exist in the Greek text but is shown in the first person singular inflection of the verb "give."

Some grammarians contend that the personal pronoun "nowhere occurs without emphasis" (Johann Winer, *Grammar*). When the pronoun is actually used in the Greek text, we must therefore expect a certain amount of emphasis, though not always of the same degree.

Determining just where the emphatic personal pronoun does or does not occur cannot be done with the ordinary English translation, due to the difference between Greek and English in this respect. However, the *Newberry Reference Bible* points out the emphatic pronoun everywhere it occurs through the use of distinctive type, and of course it is a simple matter to detect the occurrence of the pronoun by using the Greek text itself.

Examples of the emphatic personal pronoun are common:

Jesus looked at him, and said, "*You* are Simon, the son of John; *you* shall be called Cephas" (John 1:42 NASB)

I am the way, and the truth, and the life (John 14:6 NASB).

Another important feature of the pronoun lies in something that has already been considered briefly: the agreement between the relative pronoun and the noun to which it refers. An example is found in Matthew 1:16:

And to Jacob was born Joseph the husband of Mary, by whom was born Jesus, who is called Christ" (NASB).

In English the "whom" could refer either to Joseph or to Mary. Quite obviously, it makes quite a bit of difference which one it actually does refer to in this case. The matter is simple in the Greek, however. The pronoun "whom" is *hēs,* the genitive singular feminine form of *hos.* Being feminine, it refers to Mary, not to Joseph. Jesus was born "by Mary," not in any sense "by Joseph."

The Article

Also closely related to the noun is the article. "If it is desired to represent the thing designated by the noun as particular or known, we may use the *article*" (Dana and Mantey, *Manual Grammar*).

In English we have both a definite article ("the") and an indefinite article ("a" or "an"). Greek, however, has only the *definite* article and is therefore referred to simply as "the article." There are two general rules which it will be helpful for us to know when dealing with the article. These are: the *presence* of the article denotes the noun as definite or particular in some sense; and the *absence* of the article indicates the noun as either indefinite or qualitative. There are exceptions and qualifying circumstances to these rules, but these are the simplest and most common uses of the article.

As an example of the presence of the article, we have John 1:1: "In the beginning was *the* Word" (*en archē ēn ho logos*). Here John is not speaking of just "any" word, but *the* Word, Christ Himself.

The article is sometimes added to names in the New

Testament (see the genealogy in Matthew 1 in the Greek text) when the writer is referring to specific and well-known persons bearing those names.

The article is also used to show previous reference—that is, "to point out an object the identity of which is defined by some previous reference made to it in the context" (Dana and Mantey, *Manual Grammar*). For example: "Where then do You get that [literally 'the'] living water?" (John 4:11 NASB)—i.e., the water previously referred to by Jesus, in verse 10.

As an example of the absence of the article, we have John 1:6: "There came a man" (*egeneto anthrōpos*), where indefiniteness is indicated. In John 1:4, "In Him was life" (*en autō zōē ēn*), we have an example of the qualitative use of the absence of the article. In Christ was the essence of life—i.e., that which has the quality, characteristics, and nature of life itself.

Often an indefinite object is indicated by the use of "one" or "a certain" in the Greek:

He saw *one* fig-tree (Matthew 21:19)
Answered him never *one* word (Matthew 27:14)
There was in *a certain* city *a certain* judge (Luke 18:2).

A good example of the importance of determining the presence or absence of the article is found in John 17:17.

Sanctify them in the truth; Thy word is truth (NASB).

In the first part of the sentence, "truth" has the article, but in the second part, it does not. In the first instance, Christ is speaking of the particular truth revealed through Himself and His words; in the second instance, we could render: "Your word [alone] is absolutely true in nature." Only the Word of God, therefore, can sanctify us because only His Word is truth itself in its very nature.

The use of the article can easily be seen by using the Greek text with an interlinear version. Remember that the Greek article changes its basic form according to case, person, etc. The basic form of the article is *ho* for masculine, *hē* for feminine, and *to* for neuter.

The *Newberry Reference Bible* is also quite consistent in pointing out the presence and absence of the article in the original, as are most literal translations and many modern versions.

The Preposition

The class of words called prepositions are also related to nouns: "It may be desired to make the fundamental relation of the noun to its context more vivid than can be done by the devices of inflection. This purpose is served by the *preposition*" (Dana and Mantey, *Manual Grammar*).

The study of prepositions is both interesting and rewarding. A relatively complete list of the many prepositions used in the New Testament will be found in Appendix B. Here we will examine only a few of the most common ones.

The meaning of a preposition will be seen to depend to a great extent on the case of the noun with which it is used and the context where it occurs.

Some prepositions are quite similar in meaning, and most grammarians admit that in many cases they could be (and are) used interchangeably. In some situations, however, recognizing a distinction between similar prepositions can help to clarify difficult passages. For example, consider *apo, ek,* and *para,* three prepositions all having the basic meaning: "from." *Apo* is found in Matthew 3:16: "He went *up from* the water." Mark, however, records Jesus as "going *up out of* the water" (Mark 1:10) and uses *ek*. And *para* is also rendered "from" in the New Testament, as, for example, "Ask a drink *from* me" (John 4:9). What is the difference between these three words? Dana and Mantey remark, "*Apo* may include the idea expressed in *ek*, but its usual significance is *from the edge of*, while *ek* has the idea *from within*. *Para* (with the ablative case) emphasizes source and is used only with persons, as in John 9:16: *ouk estin outos para Theou*, "This one is not from God' " (*Manual Grammar*).

Another important preposition is *dia*, meaning "through, by means of." We find it, for example, in John 3:17:

That the world should be saved through [i.e., by means of] Him (NASB).

Dia may refer to a simple local "through," as in John 4:4 ("He had to pass through Samaria," NASB), or to agency or source, as in John 1:3 ("All things came into being through Him," NASB).

Two other prepositions often confused are *eis*, meaning "unto, into, in," and *en*, meaning "in." The two are very closely related. In fact, grammarians have shown that *eis* was derived from *en* and has gradually taken over its functions to the extent that *en* does not even occur in modern Greek.

Eis is used of going *unto* (motion toward) or *into and in* — i.e., resting in; *en*, on the other hand, is usually used simply of the state of being *in* a place, position, or sphere.

The distinction between *eis* and *en* can be seen from such passages as John 1:9:

There was the true light which, coming into [*eis*] the world, enlightens every man (NASB);

and John 1:4:

> In [*en*] Him was life (NASB).

Another preposition, *huper,* means basically "over." However, in some instances it is used to mean "for the sake of, on behalf of." In Titus 2:14 we have:

> He gave Himself for [i.e., on behalf of] us [or "for our sakes"].

Prepositions are not only found alone, but are found frequently in composition or compound with other words, where they usually express intensity or emphasis. For example, the preposition *ana* has the basic or root meaning of "up," but it rarely occurs alone and with this simple meaning in the New Testament. In compounds it means "up, back, again." For example, the word is found in *anakainōsis* in Romans 12:2:

> Do not be conformed to this world, but be transformed by the *renewing* of your mind (NASB).

Notice that the root of this root is *kainos,* new in quality (see the example from Trench in Chapter Eight), with the preposition *ana* indicating "new again" or renewal.

As even a casual study of prepositions as they are actually used in the New Testament will indicate, it is not possible to attach one and only one meaning to each preposition. The meaning must be derived from the context, the case with which it is used, the various usages of the preposition throughout the New Testament and Greek literature, etc.

When we realize how frequently these prepositions are used (*eis,* for example, occurs over seventeen hundred times in the New Testament), we realize how important it is to distinguish clearly between the different prepositions. The particular Greek preposition used in any specific passage can be determined easily through using the Greek text, either plain or in an interlinear version. The *Newberry Reference Bible* also points out in many cases the particular prepositions employed.

The Conjunction

"A conjunction is a word that connects sentences, clauses, phrases and words. It may be a mere colorless copulative giving no additional meaning to the words proceeding or following (as is true of *te* and is usually the case with *kai*) or it may introduce a new meaning in addition to being a connective (as is true of *hina* and *hōste*)" (Dana and Mantey, *Manual Grammar*).

Among the more common conjunctions which we will encounter are *kai, alla, gar, de, hina,* and *oun.*

Kai is the most simple and common conjunction, usually being rendered by "and." However, it can also mean "even, also." Examples abound of its various uses:

Grace to you and [*kai*] peace from God our Father and [*kai*] the Lord Jesus Christ" (2 Corinthians 1:2 NASB).

Whoever does not have, even [*kai*] what he has shall be taken away from him (Matthew 13:12 NASB).

But false prophets also [*kai*] arose among the people (2 Peter 2:1 NASB).

De and *alla* are both rendered "but" often in the New Testament. For example, *alla* is found in Matthew 5:17:

I did not come to abolish, but [*alla*] to fulfill (NASB).

De is found in Matthew 5:22:

But [*de*] I say to you (NASB).

De can also be rendered "now," as in John 7:2: "Now [*de*] the feast of the Jews . . . was at hand" (NASB). Or it can be rendered "and" (it appears thirty-eight times as "and" in the genealogy of Matthew 1). In some cases it could be rendered as either of these, depending on the context.

Gar is most commonly rendered "for," as in John 3:16: "For [*gar*] God so loved the world. . . ." *Gar* usually express-es ground, reason, explanation, confirmation, or assur-ance. It can often be rendered "because," as in Romans 1:16:

For [because] I am not ashamed of the gospel, for [because] it is the power of God for [literally, 'unto': *eis*] salvation (NASB).

Hina is used to show purpose or result. Its full meaning is "in order that" but it is usually rendered "that" in most English versions. An example is found in Matthew 7:1:

Do not judge lest you be judged yourselves [literally *in order that* you not be judged] (NASB).

Another example is Ephesians 2:10:

For we are His workmanship, created in Christ Jesus for good works, which God prepared beforehand, that [*in order that*] we should walk in them" (NASB).

This verse is also an interesting study in prepositions. Note that the first "for" is *gar,* the second "for" is *epi,* and the two "in's" are *en*; see how these distinctions which we have already learned clarify this sentence. (See Appendix B for the meaning and force of *epi,* which we did not discuss in this chapter.)

Oun is often rendered "therefore" and is important in determining sequence and chain of thoughts in the New Testament. Remember that the Bible was not written as isolated verses grouped together aimlessly. Every verse (sentence or phrase) has a vital connection with what precedes and what succeeds as well as with the overall context. As someone has remarked, "Whenever you see a 'therefore,' always find out what it's there for." Some examples are:

Therefore [*oun*: in view of what he has previously stated regarding the Word of God] . . . like newborn babes, long for the pure milk of the word (1 Peter 2:1-2 NASB).

Therefore [*oun*], since Christ has suffered in the flesh [here Peter sums up his conclusion reached in the previous section himself], arm yourselves also with the same purpose (1 Peter 4:1 NASB).

The Particle

One of the most interesting and instructive studies relates to the Greek particles. The word "particle" can actually be used to classify all of the smaller words which we have just considered, such as prepositions and conjunctions. Most grammarians, however, use the word to refer to the smaller words which are not included in the other categories, a sort of "catchall" for words which do not fit into any other category.

As Dana and Mantey remark:

The abundant and diversified uses of particles by the Greeks is one of the most unique and distinctive characteristic of this unparalleled language. However, in contrast with classical Greek we find comparatively few particles in the papyri and the New Testament. The fact that they are seldom used makes their use all the more significant, for it is evident that each occurrence of a particle was necessary to help express the writer's ideas. In them lurk hidden meanings and delicate shades of thought that intensify and clarify the thought of the sentence. Unless one learns to understand and appreciate their significance, he will miss getting the author's full thought and fail to realize the benefit of the niceties of Greek (*Manual Grammar*).

Particles can be divided into two main categories: emphatic or intensive, and negative. An example of the first type is *ge,* a word which can be rendered "at least, indeed, even, in fact." It occurs, for example, in Romans 8:32:

He who *indeed* [*ge*: note that this word is omitted in this and many versions] did not spare His own Son, but delivered Him up for us all (NASB).

As can be seen from this example, many particles are often omitted in English translations. This is why we need to learn to use the Greek text itself through Greek study aids.

Dē (be sure to distinguish this from *de* above) is another emphatic particle often left untranslated. It occurs, for example, in 1 Corinthians 6:20: "*By all means* glorify God in your body." (The word may have a climactic force here: "*therefore* glorify God.") The NASB renders *dē* as "indeed" in Matthew 13:23 and "assuredly" in Hebrews 2:16.

Men, sometimes rendered "indeed" and often left untranslated, is sometimes used with *de* (not *dē* above) and helps to distinguish two clauses or phrases, often by contrasting them and at other times simply by separating two related thoughts. Arndt and Gingrich (*Greek-English Lexicon*) suggest that the two particles can be rendered as "to be sure . . . but" or "on the one hand . . . on the other hand." An example is found in Matthew 3:11:

I, on the one hand [*men*], baptize you with water unto repentance; He, on the other hand [*de*], who is coming after me . . . will baptize you with the Holy Spirit and fire.

Another example is found in Romans 6:11:

Even so consider yourselves to be dead [on the one hand] to sin, but [on the other hand] alive to God in Christ Jesus (NASB).

There are two chief negative particles: *ou* and *mē*. There is an important, though not always realized, distinction between them. For example, when *mē* is used with a question, the expected answer is always no. The NASB Preface remarks: "In the rendering of negative questions introduced by the particle *mē* (which always expects the answer, 'No') the wording has been altered from a mere, 'Will he not do this?' to a more accurate, 'He will not do this, will he?' " An example is found in John 4:12:

You are not greater than our father Jacob, are You? (NASB).

Here the Samaritan woman expects that the answer to her question will be no. How surprised she is to learn that the true answer is *yes*!

On the other hand, when *ou* is used in a question, yes is the expected answer. *Ou* is found twice in Matthew 13:55:

Is not this the carpenter's son? Is not His mother called Mary? (NASB).

Here the citizens of Nazareth naturally expect the answer to be yes. The questions might be phrased, "After all, He is [only] the carpenter's son, isn't He? His mother is called Mary, isn't she?"

Ou and *mē* are found in the same sentence in Luke 6:39:

A blind man cannot guide a blind man, can he [*mē* = of course not]? Will they not both fall into a pit [*ou* = of course they will]? (NASB).

Ou and *mē* are found together a number of times in the New Testament as a double negative. In English, a double negative is grammatically incorrect and has the effect of making a statement positive, but in Greek it makes the negative character of the statement doubly emphatic. J. H. Moulton remarks that "*ou mē* is rare, and very emphatic in the non-literary papyri" (*Grammar of New Testament Greek*).

When *ou mē* is used in the New Testament it always expresses great emphasis. It should be rendered "by no means, certainly not, assuredly not," etc. Unfortunately, however, it is often translated by a simple negative, thus obscuring the distinction between the single and the double negative.

An example is found in Matthew 5:20:

Unless your righteousness surpasses that of the scribes and Pharisees, you shall not [i.e., *by no means*] enter the kingdom of heaven (NASB).

Another example is John 6:37:

The one who comes to Me I will *certainly not* cast out (NASB).

An intensely emphatic sentence is found in Hebrews 13:5:

I will never desert you, nor will I ever forsake you (NASB).

The Greek here reads:

By no means [*ou mē*] will I leave you nor [*oud'*] by any means [*ou mē*] will I forsake you.

To illustrate the emphasis, compare Kenneth Wuest's translation:

I will not, I will not cease to sustain and uphold you. I will not, I will not, I will not let you down (*Expanded Translation*).

Conditional Particles and Clauses

Some particles fall outside the above two categories. One such particle is *an,* a word which Bruce M. Metzger states is "an untranslatable word, the effect of which is to make a statement contingent which would otherwise be definite" (*Lexical Aids for Students of New Testament Greek*).

This particle is found, for example, in Mark 6:56:

Whoever touched Him was cured.

The Greek reads *hosoi an hēpsanto autou, esōzonto.* Notice that the *an* is not translated, but adds the idea of contingency. Here, when used with the aorist, the particle denotes repeated action in past time, but only under certain given conditions.

An is also found in Hebrews 8:4:

If He were on earth, He would not even be a priest.

The Greek reads *ei ēn epi gēs, oud' an ēn hiereus.*

Closely related to the subject of conditional particles is that of conditional clauses. Conditional clauses are common both in English and in Greek. A conditional clause is simply the statement of a supposition, "the fulfillment of which is assumed to secure the realization of a potential fact expressed in a companion clause" (Dana and Mantey, *Manual Grammar*). For example, we might say, "If it rains, I will get wet." Here the first clause (called the *protasis*) contains the supposition, while the second (called the *apodosis*) states what will happen if the first clause is fulfilled. We

often speak of such conditional sentences as "if/then" statements. Examples abound in John's First Letter (all examples from NASB):

If we say that we have fellowship with Him and yet walk in
the darkness, [*then*] we lie and do not practice the truth (1:6).

If we say that we have no sin, [*then*] we are deceiving ourselves,
and the truth is not in us (1:8).

If we say that we have not sinned, [*then*] we make Him a liar,
and His word is not in us (1:10).

In Greek, conditional clauses are divided into four basic
categories based on the attitude which each expresses with
reference to reality or probability.

1. First we have the simple or *true-to-fact* condition (known
grammatically as a first-class condition). Here there is nothing definitely stated as to whether this fact actually exists,
but for the sake of argument it is assumed to do so. An
example is found in Matthew 4:3:

If You are the Son of God, [*then*] command that these stones
become bread" (NASB).

Here Satan is neither denying nor affirming Christ's deity.
The "if " here could be rendered "since" or "in view of the
fact." The fact is *assumed* to be true for the sake of express-
ing an argumentative conclusion: "In view of the fact that
you are the Son of God, *then. . . .*"

2. The *contrary-to-fact* condition (known as a second-class
condition) implies that the fact stated has not been realized
and therefore does not exist. Here a supposition is stated
purely for the sake of showing a conclusion, even though
the supposition is known to be false. An example is found
in John 15:19:

If you were of the world, [*then*] the world would love its own (NASB).

Here Christ is simply calling attention to the fact that "If [which is not the case] you were of the world, [then naturally] the world would love its own." The point He is making, of course, is that the disciples—and all Christians—are *not* of the world, and therefore we cannot expect to receive the world's love.

3. In some cases the *protasis* clause may simply imply that the condition stated is a probability. It may be implied that there is a very good chance of this condition coming true. This is known as a *more probable* (or third-class) condition. An example is found in 1 John 1:9:

If we confess our sins, [*then*] He is faithful and righteous to forgive us our sins and to cleanse us from all unrighteousness (NASB).

Here the confessing of our sins is viewed as something that might or might not happen (though it is expressed as being a *more probable* occurrence in view of the fact that we are Christians with the indwelling Holy Spirit and are hungry to enjoy the fellowship with God); if we do confess our sins, then we will be forgiven.

4. Similar to the more probable is the *less probable* (fourth-class) condition. Here the fulfillment of the condition is viewed simply as a *possibility,* with no real implication that it might occur and in fact with the suggestion that it will *not* occur. This condition is used only rarely and never in full form in the New Testament. No complete example of this condition is found in the New Testament (complete in both clauses), and in fact A.T. Robertson claims that no example can be found in the papyri, the writings of the

"common folk" of the early Christian era. "It is an orna-
ment of the cultured class and was little used by the masses
save in a few set phrases" (*A Grammar of the Greek New
Testament*).

An example of an incomplete fourth-class condition is
found in 1 Peter 3:14:

"But even if you should suffer for the sake of righteousness,
you are blessed" (NASB).

Here Peter is envisioning suffering for righteousness' sake
as something that may or may not occur, though according
to this construction Peter's readers stood a remote possibility of suffering *in this manner*. A.T. Robertson remarks, "If
matters, in spite of the prophetic note of victory in verse
thirteen, should come to actual suffering 'for righteousness' sake,' as in Matthew 5:10, then 'blessed' (the very
word of Jesus there) are ye."

Determining just which class condition is used in a particular passage depends on a number of factors: the use of
ean or *ei* (both meaning "if "), the use of *an,* the mood of
each clause, etc. It is not always simple for the English
reader to decide just which class condition is being used,
especially in view of the fact that there are many irregular
conditional statements in the New Testament, which do
not exactly fit into either of these categories. However,
such conditions are usually pointed out by the various
word-study commentaries discussed in Chapters Six and
Eight. The reader who wishes to learn more about conditional statements, including how to identify them from the
Greek text alone, can consult any of the standard grammars listed in Appendix C.

A Final Example

We have looked at the most important vocabulary and grammatical aids relating to New Testament Greek and have considered the basic terms which we will encounter in our use of these aids. For our final example we will take a passage from the Greek New Testament itself and attempt an exegesis of it using only the tools which we have considered in this book.

For our example we will use 1 Corinthians 13:1, the Greek text of which is found on the first page of Chapter One. When you first saw this portion reproduced from the Greek New Testament, did you dream that you would be able to "read" it yourself by the time you finished this book?

Since we already have the text printed in Greek characters on that page, we will reproduce it here in English characters for convenience. For locating the words in lexicons, you can refer back to Chapter One.

Ean tais glōssais tōn anthrōpōn lalō kai tōn aggelōn, agapēn de mē echō, gegona chalkos ēchōn ē kumbalon alalazon.

Note first of all that this verse is exactly the same in the Received Text, the United Bible Societies Text, and the Nestle Text. Also, be sure to note the accent marks as placed in the Greek text on the first page of Chapter One. We have not discussed these, since the English reader can usually safely ignore them. However, there are a few instances where the only difference between two similar words is the accent: compare hē (ἡ), "the," and ē (ἤ), "or." See the first four listings under the letter "eta" for these and two other similar words in any standard lexicon.

Step One. First we will analyze the passage word by word,

then we will offer some suggestions for further study of the verse. We will not attempt to suggest every work that can be used to study this passage, nor will we be concerned with detailed procedures, since we have already discussed these in previous chapters.

At first glance you may feel that you do not recognize any of these words, but actually, of the nineteen words in this verse, we have already encountered eight of them in one form or another. In addition, five of these words have familiar English cognates, or counterparts.

First we will look at the words themselves, and then we will see how the words are used together.

Ean: Using any standard of analytical lexicon, we find that *ean* means "if." It is a conjunction (see Appendix B) and is important in determining the class of a conditional statement. Note that conjunctions, prepositions, and most other particles do not change their basic forms and can therefore be located in any standard lexicon.

Tais: This word cannot be found in alphabetical order in this form in either a standard lexicon or the almost-complete *Analytical Lexicon*. This is the dative feminine plural form of the article, the forms of which are not always listed in such works. When faced with such a situation, we can make use of an interlinear version to see the significance of the word, and then consult an article table (such as is found in the preface to the *Analytical Greek Lexicon* and most standard grammars) to determine what form the particular inflections indicate in a particular situation.

Glōssais: This word can be located in the *Analytical Lexicon* but not in a standard lexicon under this form. It can also be found in certain word-study volumes and similar works with its basic form indicated. This is true of all the major words in this passage, but not every individual word.

Glōssais is listed as the dative plural form of *glōssa*, meaning "the tongue"—i.e., "speech, talk, language," etc. Here we see that *glōssais* agrees with its article in form: both are dative plural feminine. (To discover the gender of a noun, always look at the article listed with the word in the lexicon, then compare with the article table: *ho* for masculine, *hē* for feminine, *to* for neuter.) The plural form tells us that the word is "tongues, languages." This is one of the several cognates in this passage: compare the modern glossolalia, glossary, etc.

Tōn: Again we have the article: this time it is the genitive plural form (notice that the form is the same for masculine, feminine, and neuter in the genitive plural).

Anthrōpōn: Locating this word in the *Analytical Lexicon*, we find that this is the genitive plural form (thus agreeing with its article) of *anthrōpos*, "a human being, an individual, man." Compare our word "anthropology," the study of mankind, the human race.

Lalō: This word is a verb. It can be located in the *Analytical Lexicon* or Han's *Parsing Guide*. Han, for example, tells us that the word is a first-person singular present active indicative form of *laleō*. Finding *laleō* in any lexicon, we see that it means "to make vocal utterance, to talk, to exercise the faculty of speech, to speak." The inflections tell us that it is "I speak" or "I talk" at the present time.

Kai means "and, even, also," depending on the context. Here we will see, as we progress in our examination of this passage, that it is a simple connective: "and."

Tōn we have already considered: it is the genitive plural form of the article.

Aggelōn: Locating this word in the *Analytical Lexicon*, we find that it corresponds to the previous *anthrōpōn*; i.e., it is the genitive plural form of *aggelos*, which means "one sent, a messenger, an angel." This word derives from *aggellō*, "to tell, to announce." Compare this with our word "angel." Notice that *aggelos* is pronounced *angelos* and notice also that this word occurs in *euaggelizō*, "to tell or announce the good news."

Agapēn: Locating this word in the *Analytical Lexicon*, we find that it is the accusative singular form of *agapē*, a word with which we are already familiar. *Agapē*, you will recall, is one of the two great words for "love" in the New Testament and refers to the selfless, divine love displayed in John 3:16 and which is possible in us only through the action of the Holy Spirit. This chapter—1 Corinthians 13— is of course the great "love chapter" and gives an excellent definition of *agapē*.

De is "but, and." Here we see from the context that it should be rendered adversatively, "but." Notice that it is a rule of Greek syntax that *de* never occurs first in a sentence or clause (nor does *gar*), though in English we would naturally place it first.

Mē is another word we have already studied. It means "no, not," depending on the context. Here we will see that it is best rendered "not."

Echō is another verb and can be found in the *Analytical Lexicon*. It is listed as the first-person singular present subjunctive form of *echō*, "to have, hold, possess." The inflections inform us that it should be rendered "I have." The present tense gives us progressive action, which in English could be represented as "I am having at the present time." The subjunctive shows us that there is contingency involved.

Gegona: This word can be located in the *Analytical Lexicon* or Han's *Parsing Guide*. Han lists it as the first-person singular perfect active indicative form of *ginomai*. Any standard lexicon will inform us that *ginomai* means "to come into existence, to become." The inflections inform us that the word should be rendered "I have become."

Chalkos: This word can be found in any lexicon, as it is already in its basic form. Again, however, whenever in doubt consult the *Analytical Lexicon*. This word means "copper, bronze, or a brazen musical instrument." Note that the basic position of a noun is always nominative singular. The article tells us that *chalkos* is masculine.

Ēchōn: Be sure to distinguish this word from *echō* above. They appear similar in English but are not related: note that they begin with different letters in Greek. This word can be found in either of the two works previously mentioned. We find that it is the present active participle nominative singular masculine form of the verb *ēcheō*, "to sound, ring, roar." The present participle shows us that the word is being used adjectivally of progressive action in the present time. It could be rendered "sounding." (Compare our word "echo," which derives from this word.)

Ē: Remember what we said concerning accents in regard to this word? This word means "either, or." We must pay careful attention to accent marks when locating this word in the lexicon. Since it is a conjunctive particle, it can be found in any standard lexicon.

Kumbalon: This word can also be located in any standard lexicon. Note that it appears only *once* in the New Testament and that it is already in its basic form. This means that it is nominative singular. The article informs us that it is neuter. The word means "a cymbal" (from *kumbos*, "a hollow") and comes into English as the same word: cymbal.

Alalazon: The final word is another verb (note that there are five in this verse). Locating it in either the *Analytical*

Lexicon or the *Parsing Guide,* we see that it is the present active participle nominative singular neuter form of *alalazō,* "to raise the war-cry—i.e., to utter loud sounds, to wail, tinkle, ring." This word corresponds in form to *ēchōn* above: both are present active participles and both modify nouns in their basic position: nominative singular. It is interesting to note that *alalazō* is an onomatopoeic word—i.e., a word which attempts to reproduce an abstract sound, as *buzz* in English. *Alalazō* not only *means* a "wailing, tinkling, ringing"; it actually sounds like it as well.

Now that we have analyzed all of these words, let's illustrate them conveniently as follows:

ean: "if"
tais: "the"—dat. fem. pl.
glōssais: "languages, tongues"—dat. fem. pl.
tōn: "the"—gen. pl.
anthrōpōn: "man, mankind"—gen. pl.
lalō: "speak, talk"—1 p. sg. pres. act. ind.
kai: "and"
tōn: "the"—gen. pl.
aggelōn: "angel, messenger"—gen. pl.
agapēn: "love"—acc. sg.
de: "but, and"
mē: "not, no"
echō: "have, hold"—1 p. sg. pres. act. subj.
gegona: "become"—1 p. sing. perf. act. ind.
chalkos: "bronze, brazen musical instrument"—nom. sing. masc.
ēchōn: "roar, ring, sound"—pres. act. ptc. nom. sg. masc.
ē: "either, or"
kumbalon: "cymbal"—nom. sing. neut.
alalazon: "tinkle, ring"—pres. act. ptc. nom. sg. neut.

Step Two. Reading the sentence exactly as we have it thus

far, we get the following: "If the languages the men speak and the angels, love but not have, have become bronze sounding or cymbal tinkling."

Now let's look at some clues which point out the relations between these words. The first "the" (*tais*) is dative feminine plural and obviously modifies "languages." Similarly, the second "the" (*ton*) agrees with "men" and the third "the" agrees with "angels." The dative—"the languages"—determines the character of this phrase and could be rendered "in the languages." The genitives could be rendered "of the men, of the angels."

The first-person singular form of the verb "speak" indicates Paul (i.e., the writer) as the speaker. The entire first phrase, therefore, can be rendered: "If I speak in the languages of the men and of the angels."

The second phrase consists of four words: "love but not have." Since *de* never comes first in Greek, but should be placed first in English, we can render: "but love. . . ." The "have" is first-person singular present: "I have." The entire phrase could be rendered idiomatically: "but I have not love" or "but I do not have love."

The third phrase consists of a verb—"I have become"—and two parallel phrases. Note that "sounding" (nominative singular masculine) obviously modifies "bronze" while "tinkling" obviously modifies "cymbal." The entire phrase could read, "I have become sounding bronze [or a sounding brazen musical instrument] or a tinkling cymbal."

Notice that we have examples of the dative, genitive, accusative, and nominative cases. Notice also that in arriving at this translation we have been forced to choose between the various definitions for certain words, a procedure that is always necessary and is dependent on context, etc. This is one of the factors which keeps any two translations from being exactly the same.

Step Three. Having arrived at an analysis of the Greek text, let's now look at some approaches to further study.

1. Note the conditional sentence: "*If* I speak . . . but [yet] have not love, [*then*] I have become. . . ." The use of *ean* and the present subjunctive in the protasis indicates that this is a third-class construction—i.e., a *more probable* condition. As A.T. Robertson remarks, it is a "supposable case." We might illustrate this in this manner: "Suppose that I *could* speak with the languages of men and even of angels, but yet I didn't have love, what would be the result? I would be no better than the empty jangling sounds produced by sounding brass and a tinkling cymbal."

2. Two words, *ēchōn* and *alalazōn,* appear only twice in the New Testament. In addition to here, *ēchōn* appears in Luke 21:25:

And there will be . . . perplexity at the *roaring* of the sea and the waves (NASB).

Alalazōn also appears in Mark 5:38:

And they came to the house of the synagogue official; and He beheld a commotion, and people loudly weeping and *wailing* (NASB).

Kumbalon, as we have noted, is another rare word, appearing only in this passage.

3. Other words interesting for study are *chalkos* (note that it appears in Matthew 10:9 and Revelation 18:12, where it is rendered "brass" in the KJV, and in Mark 6:8 and 12:41, where it is rendered "money" in the KJV), and *glōssa.* The latter word occurs some fifty times in the New Testament and is also translated "tongue" in the King James Version. *Agapē* is of course a very important word, and one of the best passages in the New Testament for the study of this word is this very chapter, 1 Corinthians 13.

4. Now read the comments on this verse in one of the word-study volumes such as *Vincent* or *Robertson*. For example, Robertson remarks that " 'Intellect was worshipped in Greece, and power in Rome; but where did St. Paul learn the surpassing beauty of love?' Whether Paul had ever seen Jesus in the flesh, he knows Him in the spirit. One can substitute Jesus for love all through this panegyric" (*Word Pictures*).

We can also compare other translations and, by having analyzed the verse ourselves, come to a greater appreciation and understanding of the various differences between different versions. For example, Young renders the passage as:

If with the tongues of men and of messengers I speak, and have not love, I have become brass sounding, or a cymbal tinkling" (*Literal Translation*).

Wuest, on the other hand, renders:

If in the languages of men I speak and the languages of the angels but do not have love, I have already become and at present am sounding brass or a clanging cymbal" (*Expanded Translation*).

Obviously, an approach to a Bible passage cannot always be this detailed. Lack of time alone, if nothing else, would prevent such a detailed analysis of every verse that we study. Ordinarily we would concentrate on the important distinctions and words presented. Here the most interesting features include Paul's use of the third-class condition (what does this imply about Paul's statement?) and the unusual reference to musical sounds and instruments. The most important thing to remember, however, has to do not with Greek grammar, syntax, or vocabulary, but with love. Paul's consideration of this great topic in this and the following few verses is simply: "Without love I am nothing. No matter what I have, or what I can do, or who I am, without love I am nothing at all." What a lesson for us today! Though we might be the world's richest man, the world's most devout person, the world's greatest preacher or evangelist, or the world's most devoted missionary, yet if we do not have love—true, genuine love in the highest sense for God, for others, even for ourselves—then we are nothing!

Suggestions for Further Study

Now that we have considered the first verse of 1 Corinthians 13, why not "practice" on the remaining verses of this brief but important chapter? Simply use the procedures which we have noted: make a basic study of the passage, using the vocabulary and grammatical aids we have considered; concentrate on important words and unusual features; follow up with a study of the comments on this passage by various English word-study writers, etc. Finally, we might consider the chapter in a more technical work such as *Alford's* or *Expositor's*. We might also consider the synonyms which we will encounter in Trench's *Synonyms*, etc. For example, what is the difference between *laleō* ("to speak") found in verse 1 and *legō*, another word for "speak" found in the New Testament?

To help us get started, the following is a brief analysis of the second verse (note that words repeated in the verse are not repeated here). What conclusions can we draw from the information supplied in the light of what we have already learned? What words deserve fuller treatment? What grammatical insights can we discover on our own?

kai: "and"

ean: "if "

echō: "have, hold, possess"—1 p. sing. pres. subj. act.

prophēteian: "prophecy"—acc. sing. fem. (*prophēteia*)

eidō: "know"—1 p. sing. perf. act. subj. (*oida*)

ta: "the"—nom. or acc. pl. neut.

mustēria: "secret, mystery"—acc. pl. neut. (*mustērion*)

panta: "all, every"—acc. pl. neut. (*pas*)

pasan: "all, every"—acc. sing. fem. (*pas*)

tēn: "the"—acc. sing. fem.

gnōsin: "knowledge"—acc. sing. fem. (*gnōsis*)

pistin: "faith, belief "—acc. sing. fem. (*pistis*)

hōste: "so that, so as that, so as to"

orē: "mountain, hill"—nom. and acc. pl. neut. (*oros*)

methistanai: "to remove"—pres. act. infin. (*methistēmi*)

agapēn: "love"—acc. sing. fem. (*agapē*)

de: "but, and"

mē: "no, not"

outhen: "not one, no one, nothing"—nom. sing. neut.(*outheis*)

eimi: "to be, to exist"—1 p. sing. pres. act. ind. (*eimi*)

12

GO FORWARD!

In this chapter we will consider some miscellaneous uses of Greek study aids and also voice a few warnings and cautions in regard to their use.

We have now considered all of the basic types of aids used not only by laymen but also by pastors, teachers, and scholars. Some of these aids can be used with little effort. These works (which include the concordances and English word studies) should be approached first by the beginner.

As we gain familiarity with the Greek alphabet, we will find it simple to locate words in a lexicon. By understanding the basic differences between Greek and English grammar, we can begin to make use of grammatical aids. Soon we will be using the Greek Testament itself with only a small amount of effort.

What next? Where do we go from here? Remember that what we have learned in this book is only a beginning. The study of the Greek New Testament—indeed, the study of the Bible in *any* language—is a lifelong affair. The more we learn, the more we realize how little we really have learned! The skills we develop in learning to make use of these study aids will stand us in good stead the rest of our days and will immeasurably enrich our devotional and Christian lives. This is true whether we preach, teach, or simply study for our own benefit.

The Old Testament

But don't stop here! If we have come this far, we have made a good beginning, but there is much more to learn. As God said to Moses at the passage of the Red Sea, "Tell the sons of Israel to *go forward*" (Exodus 14:15 NASB). There is a large portion of the Bible which we have not considered—thirty-nine of the Bible's sixty-six books, in fact.

Can Greek study aids help us in our study of the Old Testament as well as the New Testament? Yes, in several ways. First is the fact that by gaining experience with Greek study aids we will be better able to learn to use Hebrew study aids. The Old Testament was written originally in Hebrew, and Hebrew has traditionally been regarded as more difficult for the layman to master. (The Hebrew language itself is not actually more difficult. The only real obstacle for laymen lies in the unfamiliarity of the characters of the Hebrew alphabet, which are not nearly as similar to the characters of the English alphabet as are those of the Greek language.) This is one reason why we have concentrated on Greek study aids. After we have mastered the use of Greek aids, we will find it no problem to do the same with Hebrew study aids. In fact, the procedures discussed in this book (except for those dealing with grammar) can be applied directly to the field of Hebrew study tools. However, it should be pointed out that there are far fewer aids available for the lay student of the Hebrew Old Testament than for the student of New Testament Greek.

Of course, *Strong's* and *Young's* concordances can be used exactly the same way with the information they provide on the Hebrew Bible as on the Greek Testament. In addition, the beginning student can make use of such aids as the *Englishman's Hebrew and Chaldee Concordance* (Zondervan; an edition published by Associated Publishers and Authors is keyed to the numbers in *Strong's Concordance*). Other helpful works for the beginner include R.B. Girdlestone's *Synonyms of the Old Testament* and the *Analytical Hebrew and Chaldee Lexicon*. A brief list of such works will be found in Appendix C.

For one brief example of Hebrew words, let's take the word "love." We are familiar with *agapē* and *philos* in the New Testament. According to *Young's Concordance,* a number of Hebrew words are rendered "love" in the Old Testament. Among these are the following:

1. *ahabah,* "love," occurs in such passages as Genesis 29:20 (of Jacob's love for Rachel); 2 Samuel 1:26 (of Jonathan's love for David); and Zephaniah 3:17 (of God's love for Israel).

2. *ahabim* refers to "acts of love" and is found in Proverbs 7:18: "Come . . . let us solace ourselves with loves."

3. *dod* is used of the "offices of love" and is found in Proverbs 7:18 ("let us take our fill of love"), Song of Solomon 1:2 ("thy love is better than wine"), etc.

Another way in which New Testament Greek can help us with the Old Testament is this: there is a Greek version of the Old Testament known as the Septuagint. This translation (usually abbreviated as LXX) was made, according to tradition, around the third century B.C. by a group of seventy (or seventy-two, according to some authorities) Jewish scholars in Alexandria, Egypt. The legends behind this version are numerous. For example, some say that each translator was shut into a separate cell and that all the translators by divine inspiration made their versions word-for-word alike.

Ferdinand Hitzig, the Bible critic and Hebraist, was accustomed to telling his classes, "Gentlemen, have you a Septuagint? If not, sell all you have, and buy a Septuagint." Yet, despite the great importance of the LXX in our studies of both the Old and New Testaments, there are only a few aids related to the Septuagint for English readers. This is because the LXX is a version, not an original writing itself. In some places the translation is quite good, while in other places it is not very good at all. One of the main benefits of the LXX is in regard to Old Testament textual criticism. It is obvious that in many passages the translators were working from different Hebrew texts from the ones we have available today.

The aids chiefly available and usable by the English reader are *The Septuagint: Greek and English,* with an English translation by Sir Launcelot Lee Brenton, and the *Concordance of the Septuagint.* There is also an English translation of the LXX by Charles Thomson.

You may have noticed already that a number of works on New Testament Greek make constant reference to this ancient translation. Especially concerned with comparisons with the LXX are Barclay's *New Testament Words* and Cremer's *Biblico-Theological Lexicon.* Girdlestone's *Synonyms of the Old Testament* is also very valuable for the student of the LXX because Girdlestone spends about as much time and space for comments on this Greek version as he does for the original Hebrew words. Girdlestone makes quite a convincing case in his preface when he argues that it is essential for us to understand the relationship between the

LXX and the New Testament if we are truly to understand the New Testament itself. This is because many of the Greek words employed in the New Testament first gained their peculiar theological connotations in the LXX.

One of the most interesting facts about the Septuagint is this: Have you ever wondered why some quotes in the New Testament do not read quite the same way as in the passages being quoted from the Old Testament? One reason is because the New Testament writers sometimes quoted from the Septuagint rather than from the Hebrew text. (In some cases they seem to be offering their own translations or free paraphrases.) For example, Hebrews 1:6 is a direct quote from the LXX version of Deuteronomy 32:43: "And let all the angels of God worship Him." The Greek in both cases is exactly the same: *kai proskunēsatōsan autō pantes aggeloi Theou.* Most existing Hebrew texts do not have this phrase, although the Dead Sea Scrolls do contain a copy of Deuteronomy 32:43 with this phrase in Hebrew. This suggests that the LXX may have been translated from a Hebrew text other than the ones we presently possess.

Perhaps one of the most interesting and simple studies for the English reader is to use the *Concordance of the Septuagint* and *The Septuagint: Greek and English* to see where some of the great New Testament words with which we have become familiar are used in the LXX.

For example, let's take the word "grace" (Greek *charis*) and see some of the passages where *charis* occurs in the LXX version of the Old Testament. In most cases, *charis* is the rendering of the Hebrew *chen,* a word which refers to an act of love done without any expectation of a return or reward (deriving from *chanan,* "to show favor"). *Charis* is found, for example, in:

Genesis 6:8: Noah found *favor* in the eyes of the Lord (NASB).

Ruth 2:2: And Ruth ... said to Naomi, "Please let me go to the field and glean among the ears of grain after one in whose sight I may find *favor*" (NASB).

Psalm 45:2: Thou are fairer than the sons of men; *Grace* is poured upon Thy lips; Therefore God has blessed Thee forever (NASB).

Psalm 84:11: For the Lord God is a sun and shield; the Lord gives *grace* and glory (NASB).

Zechariah 4:7: What are you, O great mountain? Before Zerubbabel you will become a plain; and he will bring forth the top stone with shouts of "*Grace, grace* to it!" (NASB).

Warnings and Cautions

When W.E. Vine first issued his popular *Expository Dictionary of New Testament Words,* he remarked in the preface, "A criticism may be raised in regard to a work like this that it would provide students who know little or nothing of the original with an opportunity of airing some knowledge of Greek."

Such criticism has always been directed against works which seek to encourage laymen to discover for themselves the beauties and benefits of the Biblical originals. Is such a criticism justified? The answer is both yes and no.

Unfortunately, a great deal of damage can be done and has been done by persons who have only a superficial knowledge of the original languages. Harold J. Berry (writing in *Witnessing to the Cults,* Back to the Bible Broadcast) points out this fact when he remarks concerning the cultists that:

Others [of the cultists] may appeal to a superior knowledge of the Scriptures. Typical of this group are those who have a

secondhand knowledge of the original languages, but who appear as linguistic authorities when discussing particular passages.
Knowledge of Hebrew and Greek reveals fine shades of meaning, but it is rare that these languages give an altogether different
meaning from that of good English translations. It is also important to realize that individual words take on shades of meaning
from the context in which they are used. Therefore, although a
person might charge that one cannot properly understand the
Bible without a knowledge of Hebrew and Greek, it is also true
that one cannot properly understand the Bible even with a knowledge of Hebrew and Greek if he does not know what a given
context teaches.

To illustrate how this is true is not really necessary, as
most of us are familiar with the "proof-texters," those who
attempt to prove their particular viewpoints by minute
examinations of scattered verses placed in an apparently
random order. It should again be pointed out that the
purpose of using study aids for the English reader is *not* to
be able to devise new systems of theology or new translations of the Bible, or to prove the traditional interpretations of the Bible wrong, or to become independent of all
translations and the opinions of Bible scholars, or to become a self-taught expert in the Bible, but simply to be able
to make better and more efficient use of translations, commentaries, study guides, Sunday school books, and even
sermons, all of which abound in insight for those willing
to seek it out.

However, the criticism we have mentioned is not entirely justified, for this reason: a person who intends to twist
or pervert the Scriptures to prove his own peculiar viewpoints is going to do so *regardless* of the number of laymen's aids available. In fact, the widespread circulation of
such works as Vine's and others does not encourage such

misuse of the originals but instead enables those on the receiving end of such tactics to be better prepared to deal with such plausible-sounding arguments. It is an obvious fact that the *more* we know about the Bible, especially in the original writings, the less likely we are to be taken in by new and radical interpretations of it.

Will learning how to use the Greek New Testament on our own make us independent of all outside opinions? No, of course not. But it will certainly help us to determine wisely which works are genuinely honest and helpful in their treatments of God's sacred Word.

However, there are some cautions that we need to remember in dealing with the Greek New Testament. First, remember that our treatment of this vast subject has been quite simplified, general, and introductory. There are many rules and exceptions to the rules which we have not covered but which are fully explained in the works which we have suggested for further study.

Secondly, beware of those who propose strikingly new interpretations of Scripture on the basis of Greek words and grammar alone. Interpretation of the Bible depends on far more than just a study of the original languages. It depends principally on a vital connection with the Author of the Book and a continual dependence on the Holy Spirit.

In dealing with such radical arguments, interpretations, and translations of the Bible, there are three basic types of dangers which the reader would do well to be able to recognize. These are (1) a claim to definitiveness and perfection, with a disdain for all previous versions and interpretations of the Bible (except for those which support their particular theory, of course); (2) a claim to having discovered "at last" the *true* meaning of the Scriptures; and

(3) using human logic rather than scientific methods as a starting point for translation or interpretation.

In contrast, a responsible version such as the *Amplified New Testament* admits in its introduction that "there never has been, nor can be, an entirely adequate translation of the New Testament from the original Greek."

Dr. James Moffatt (in the preface to the revised and final edition of *The Bible: A New Translation*) states that "translation may be a fascinating task, yet no discipline is more humbling. You may be translating oracles, but you soon learn the risk and folly of posing as an oracle yourself. If your readers are dissatisfied at any point, they may be sure that the translator is still more dissatisfied with himself, if not there, then elsewhere—all the more so, because in the nature of the case he has always to appear dogmatic in print."

Every honest translator admits the enormity of his task and the impossibility of ever achieving perfection. William Barclay remarks in the foreword to his *Translation of the New Testament* that "no one ever made a translation without the haunting sense of how much better it might have been, and of the imperfections of this translation no one is more conscious than I am. I can but pray that in spite of its inadequacy it may shed for some readers a clearer light on the book which is the Word of God to men."

We should also beware of any interpretation or argument which marshals a vast array of Greek "facts" to support a particular conclusion. As we have seen, the Greek language is far more complex than many people realize. To *prove* anything by such means is standard procedure for certain cultists, but most Christians realize that there are many points of difference in New Testament interpretation (which result in the many differences between denominations—primarily in the area of church order and organization) which cannot be settled or proven one way or another by Greek exegesis. Every major doctrinal position has had adherents among the great Greek scholars of the past and present. Our great scholars have come from every major denomination (though few or none from the ranks of the cults!).

Another faulty and misleading approach noticed many times in such works is oversimplification. It is a common error of those who have not studied other languages to assume that you can render from one language into another *exactly* and *word for word,* as though solving a cryptogram—a "coded message." Some will try to convince us that every word in Greek has one and only one exact equivalent in English, and similarly in regard to grammatical terms and conditions. Now certainly we would not want to take a Greek present tense and change it into anything else, but the question is this: what does a Greek present *equal* in English? We must remember to take into account the ways in which the English language has changed over the years as it has evolved from older languages. Even our tense structure is not the same as it was one thousand years ago.

What can we do about such tactics which misuse Greek and Hebrew "facts"? The best thing is simply to be aware of the original languages of the Bible, how complex they are, and how to make use of laymen's aids in order to understand them ourselves on at least an elementary level. The only antidote for ignorance is knowledge. One of the reasons why various cultic groups have gained so many converts from traditional Christianity is simply the abysmal ignorance of what Christianity really *is* that exists in the minds of many Christians and churchgoers.

As Christians we have an awesome responsibility to grow in knowledge and truth and grace of our Lord and Saviour Jesus Christ. This can be done in no better way than through deep, intense, Spirit-led study of the Book which God has so graciously given us. Does our study have to be in the original languages of Hebrew and Greek? Of course not! *Any* language in the world can be used to communicate God's timeless and infinite message. But since God has so abundantly blessed us with tools and opportunities to discover the vast and incredible riches of His original writings, we certainly should be thankful for these incredible blessings and should make use of them to live a deeper, fuller, and more truly Christlike life.

All Scripture is inspired by God, and useful for teaching, for reproof, for correction, for training in doing what is right, so that the man of God may be perfectly fit, thoroughly equipped for every good enterprise (2 Timothy 3:16-17 Williams).

Thank God, then, for His indescribable generosity to you! (2 Corinthians 9:15 Phillips).

APPENDIX A

For Preachers and Teachers

The question may now be asked, Of what practical use is this ability to use Greek study aids and the Greek New Testament in my work for the Lord as pastor, preacher, evangelist, Sunday school teacher, etc.?

The simplest answer is that being able to work from the originals, even if slowly and with effort, will greatly improve our grasp of the Bible. The difference it will make in our endeavors for Christ should be noticeable by all.

The ability to work from the originals is *essential* if we are to expound clearly, rather than confound, the Scriptures. This is especially true for preachers, as they are generally expected to be competent in dealing with Scriptural matters. Andrew W. Blackwood, the great speaker and preaching innovator, pointed out that the preacher should always do his basic work and studies in the original tongue of the Bible (*Expository Preaching for Today*).

The ability to do exegesis from the original languages is more important for *preparation* for preaching than for preaching itself. For example, let's take Romans 5:1:

Therefore having been justified by faith, we have peace with God through our Lord Jesus Christ" (NASB).

A preacher might use this verse as a springboard for a sermon on justification. A typical outline might be:

1. the meaning of justification (declared righteous before God);
2. the means of justification (by faith);
3. the result of justification (peace with God).

What's wrong with such an outline? Nothing, really; a good preacher might take such an outline and present a sound, Biblical, inspiring, truly helpful message on justification. But such an approach is not being quite honest with the text itself. Grammatically, it is obvious from the use of the aorist participle that the thrust and emphasis of this particular verse is not "justification" at all, but *peace with God*! The primary sentence is seen from the use of the simple present tense of the verb "have": "Therefore we have peace with God." The phrase dealing with justification is actually subordinate and might be illustrated as "Therefore (having been justified by faith) we have peace with God." A sermon which dealt honestly with this text, therefore, would deal with peace and not justification. There are any number of good texts and passages in the New Testament to use when dealing with justification, but this is not one of them (unless, of course, it is taken as a part of a larger context).

A minor detail? Perhaps, but it is such minor details that make the difference between a preacher who simply *uses* the Bible and one who genuinely *expounds* it. A preacher is first and foremost one who actually exposes or expounds the Bible as the mind and will of God for the people of today. A preacher *must* be an expositor, or else he will be little more than an entertainer. Yet exposition must always begin with exegesis, and exegesis—to be worth anything at all—must always be based on the original languages.

We see, therefore, the obvious need of being able to

make use of the Greek New Testament—through tools and aids, if not directly—in our preparation for teaching and preaching.

But how much use can we make of our knowledge of Greek in our actual teaching and preaching? This depends a great deal on the congregation or class and the circumstances. Study the great sermons of the past and you will find that the greatest expositors were quite sparing with the information they gave out on such matters in the actual delivery of their sermons. We do not wish to be like the pastor of whom one in his congregation remarked, "If he doesn't Greek-root you to death, he will Hebrew-stem you to death."

However, we do have a responsibility to introduce our congregations and classes to the great riches of the original Biblical languages. We must not cultivate an aura of mystery or intellectualism when dealing with these great treasures.

But how can we best introduce laymen to the Greek New Testament and the Hebrew Bible?

1. First and foremost is a positive attitude. *Don't* get the impression that everyone will think New Testament Greek is dry as dust. I have found, in my own experience, a great interest in the originals of the Bible among laymen of all backgrounds. In many cases this interest is simple curiosity, but this curiosity can be used constructively to further Bible knowledge.

2. Make sure that your class or congregation is familiar with the history of the English Bible. This is an essential foundation to lay. Ninety percent of the friction regarding modern translations could not have come about if everyone had been better informed about the long process by which our English Bible came into being. Periodically the

history of the English Bible (beginning with the original autographs) could be reviewed (perhaps in connection with "Bible Sunday" or some other special event). Films, charts, and other materials relating to this interesting subject can be obtained from the American Bible Society as well as other sources.

All Christians should be aware that the Bible was not originally written in English. We have only to cite the case of the lady who expressed a preference for the King James Version on the ground that "if it were good enough for Paul, it's good enough for me" to realize that there are still some people who do not understand this fact.

Provide copies of the Hebrew Old Testament and Greek New Testament for a display. In addition, have other ancient versions if possible (Syriac, Latin, etc.), and as many modern versions as you can locate. Some older English versions (Tyndale, Geneva, etc.) would also be interesting.

3. Try teacher training sessions. In such classes, as well as in Sunday school classes, a pastor or teacher can make more use of his Greek knowledge than is possible in sermons. One good idea is to have a brief Greek class for teachers. Several sessions could be taken up discussing the various aids available (most of which should be available in the church library) and how to relate these aids and this information to individual classes.

Many churches are developing the habit of inviting interested persons to an informal postsermon discussion of the topics contained in the Sunday evening message. These talks are usually held in the fellowship hall. Where time permits, such a practice could be handled between pastors and teachers or pastors and congregations. Variations on such a theme are endless and, particularly if a chalkboard is available, the speaker can show why he interpreted his basic text the way he did. The result, in most cases, is not only more-informed people, but more-interested ones. Also, a better rapport is established between preacher and congregation as he explains the reasoning and background work behind his message rather than cultivating an air of mystery. Such sessions, if handled properly, generally result in more confidence in the Biblical skills of the preacher on the part of the congregation.

Needless to say, we are not advocating that the entire church be turned into a seminary or Greek institute. The Greek portion of any session—whether for teachers, congregation, or other groups—should occupy only a brief portion of the overall time. The majority of the time must be spent in relating the message of the Bible to the people of today.

4. How about teachers and their classes? Using Greek knowledge in such situations is actually much easier than might be imagined. By use of a chalkboard, the teacher (working with a small number of students—often with a regular group) can make use of Greek study aids to a wide extent.

It has been found that most students, of all ages and all backgrounds, are fascinated by getting a look at the "originals" of the Bible. After preliminary explanations and a display of the Hebrew Bible and Greek New Testament, the teacher can begin to use study aids in class regularly by letting the class get involved. Anyone can learn to use *Strong's* and other concordances, *Vine's Dictionary,* simple word-study volumes, and other works with only a little help from the teacher and a brief trial-and-error process.

Go slow, don't rush, and don't get into too many details. Start with individual words and especially those with an interesting meaning which is rather hard to render adequately in English (or else the class will see little point in studying the Greek).

5. A variation on this theme is the "Greek class." Ask for volunteers to form a class to study the Greek New Testament for a quarter or a shorter session. First an introduction should be made of the background and history of New Testament Greek, then a consideration of the aids to be employed.

Choose an entire book to study if possible, preferably one of the briefest, such as 2 or 3 John or Philemon. This approach is usually preferable to taking brief or unrelated passages because it gives the student a chance to connect the various lessons together in a practical manner, and the student will have more of a sense of accomplishment by completing an entire book in the Greek New Testament, even if it is a brief one.

Certainly such classes should never be used to form cliques of any sort. The entire thing should be voluntary and informal. The object of such studies is to penetrate the aura of mystery that surrounds the original languages of the Bible in the minds of many people so that they will be more aware of the basis of the New Testament, the differences in modern translations, the use of "Greek facts" by cultists and others, etc. In addition, the student will gain not only more *knowledge* of the New Testament but more *interest* in it. Studies have shown that such classes as these have sparked interest in persons long indifferent to the Bible.

The following is a sample outline of a six-week course in 2 John in the Greek New Testament, along with some general hints for approaching such a course. The outline can be modified to fit individual circumstances.

Second John in the Greek New Testament

First Week. Introduction to Greek New Testament and Biblical languages in general; historical background of New Testament Greek; John's writings in general; introduction to the simpler study aids, etc.

Second Week. Verses 1 and 2: two great words: love (*agapē*), and truth (*alētheia*); some interesting word studies: elect, elder, children (with synonyms), know (with synonyms); emphasis on individual words *alone,* not syntax.

Third Week. Verse 3: three great words: grace (*charis*), mercy (*eleos*), peace (*eirēnē*); an interesting word: son (cf. children above); prepositions: *para, en, meta*; begin consideration of simple syntax: simple phrases formed by the use of prepositions.

Fourth Week. Verses 4-6: consideration of word roots: cf. rejoice with grace above; interesting words: walking, commandment; conjunctions: *kai, nun*; prepositions: *apo, hina, kata*; the Greek article: *hē agapē, hē entolē,* etc.; further consideration of syntax in regard to conjunctions, cases, gender, etc.

Fifth Week. Verses 7-11: some interesting word studies: deceivers, world (compare synonyms), confess, teaching; more prepositions and conjunctions: *eis, hoti*; Greek negatives: *mē*—compare with *ou*; begin simple consideration of the Greek verb: aorist, present, participle, etc.

Sixth Week. Verses 12-13: some interesting word studies: hoping, joy, paper, ink; continue consideration of the Greek verb: perfect tense, the infinitive, the indicative and subjunctive moods; review.

Some hints for teaching and approaching the course.

1. Have each student come prepared with either an interlinear version or a Greek New Testament which can be marked interlinearly as the course proceeds.

2. Don't go into too much detail; don't try to cover every single word or every situation which occurs; this is an introduction not a seminary course.

3. Allow the students to get involved by using various aids themselves; compare (through concordances, etc.) other Scriptures where these words occur.

4. Explain English cognates to provoke interest and aid memory: *patēr*/pater; *didachē*/didactic, etc. Also point out similarity of names, such as Jesus Christ in Greek and English, and relation between *Theos* (God) and theology, etc.

5. Concentrate on *practical* teaching which can result from a study of 2 John in the Greek New Testament: for example, "going forward" in verse 9 (*proagōn*), rendered "transgresseth" in KJV; compare New International Version: "anyone who runs ahead and does not continue in the doctrine of Christ."

APPENDIX B

Miscellaneous Greek Charts

Chart 1: The Greek Alphabet

Greek Character		Name	English Equivalent
A	α	alpha	a
B	β	beta	b
Γ	γ	gamma	g
Δ	δ	delta	d
E	ε	epsilon	e
Z	ζ	zeta	z
H	η	eta	ē
Θ	θ	theta	th
I	ι	iota	i
K	κ	kappa	k
Λ	λ	lambda	l
M	μ	mu	m
N	ν	nu	n
Ξ	ξ	xi	x
O	o	omicron	o
Π	π	pi	p
P	ρ	rho	r
Σ	σ,ς	sigma	s
T	τ	tau	t
Υ	υ	upsilon	u
Φ	φ	phi	ph
X	χ	chi	ch
Ψ	ψ	psi	ps
Ω	ω	omega	ō
ʽ		rough breathing	h
ʼ		smooth breathing	silent

Chart 2: The Greek Verb

Tenses (in regard to the indicative mood only)

Present: progressive action in present time

Imperfect: progressive action in past time, or repeated or habitual action

Aorist: action considered as a simple event without reference to progress or completion

Future: undefined action in future time; with or without reference to progress or completion depending on context

Perfect: present state resulting from past action; emphasis on results rather than action

Pluperfect: past state resulting from past action

Future Perfect: future state resulting from future action occurring at a time previous to that state

Moods (most general use only)

Indicative: simple statement or question of fact

Subjunctive: uncertainty, contingency

Imperative: commands or exhortations

Optative: wishes, prayers

Voices

Active: subject *performs* the action

Passive: subject *receives* the action

Middle: subject *participates* in results of action

Related Verbal Forms

Participle: a verbal adjective

Infinitive: a verbal noun

Chart 3: The Greek Noun

Cases (Most general use only)

Nominative: subject

Genitive: possession, source, apposition, comparison, etc.

Dative: indirect object, reference

Accusative: direct object

Chart 4: Prepositions

Preposition	Basic Meaning	Related Meanings
ana	up	with the accusative: throughout, apiece
anti	against	with the genitive: in place of, instead of, on behalf of, in exchange for
apo	from	with the genitive: away from
dia	through	with the genitive: through, by means of
		with the accusative: on account of
eis	into	with the accusative: unto, in, with regard to, for the purpose of
ek	out of	with the genitive: from, by means of, out of
en	in	with the dative: in, among, at, when
epi	upon	with the genitive: upon, at the time of
		with the dative: at, upon
		with the accusative: to, upon, at
kata	down	with the genitive: against, by, down, throughout
		with the accusative: according to, by
meta	with	with the genitive: with
		with the accusative: after
para	alongside	with the genitive: from beside, from
		with the dative: beside, with
		with the accusative: alongside of, at, beyond, contrary to
peri	around	with the genitive: about, concerning
		with the accusative: about, around
pro	before	with the genitive: before, in front of, above

pros	towards	with the dative: at
		with the accusative: to, toward, at, with, in the presence of, pertaining to, for the purpose of
sun	with	with the dative: with, together with
huper	over	with the genitive: in behalf of, for the sake of, concerning, with reference to
		with the accusative: above, beyond, more than
hupo	under	with the genitive: by, by means of
		with the accusative: under

Chart 5: Conjunctions

Conjunction	Meanings
alla	but, however, certainly
ara	therefore, really
achri	until
gar	for, now
de	and, but, now, indeed
dio	wherefore
dioti	because
ean	if
ei	if
epei	when, since, otherwise
epeidē	when, since
hina	in order that, so that, that
kathōs	according to, according as
kai	and, also, even
mentoi	however, indeed
hopōs	in order that
hote	when
hoti	because, that
oun	therefore, however, now really
plēn	nevertheless
prin	before
te	and
toinun	therefore
hōs	when, as, since, in order that
hōste	so that, therefore

Chart 6: Particles

Particle	Meanings
amēn	truly, verily
an	ever (suggests vagueness, uncertainty, usually untranslated)
ge	at least, indeed, even, in fact
dē	by all means, really
ei mēn	above all, assuredly, certainly
mēn	indeed, in fact, on the one hand
nē, nai	yes, yea
per	indeed, really, completely
pote	ever, at that time, once, formerly, at length
pou, pōs	somehow, about, at all, by any means
toi	let me tell you, surely
ou	no, not
mē	no, not

APPENDIX C

Suggested Reading List

In the following list each work is listed according to title, author, and publisher, with brief explanatory comments. Following this listing is a number: a number 1 indicates that the work is suitable for the beginner with no previous knowledge of New Testament Greek; a number 2 indicates works which require some amount of familiarity with New Testament Greek, but not necessarily extensive knowledge; a number 3 refers to scholarly works intended for Greek readers and students but usable by the English reader by means of the procedures described in this book.

Concordances

English and English-Greek Concordances

Analytical Concordance to the Revised Standard Version, New Testament, Clinton Morrison, Westminster Press. An analytical concordance for those who prefer the RSV; 1.

Critical Lexicon and Concordance to the English and Greek New Testament, E.W. Bullinger, Zondervan. Lists every English word in the New Testament, with Greek words from which each is translated and passages in which they occur. 1

The Layman's English-Greek Concordance, James Gall, Baker. Similar to the above work but less extensive in scope and less expensive in price. Perfect for the beginner. 1

Strong's Exhaustive Concordance of the Bible, James Strong, Abingdon, MacDonald, Crusade, others. The standard work, concerned with both Hebrew and Greek words. Contains small but helpful Hebrew and Greek lexicons. 1

Young's Analytical Concordance to the Bible, Robert Young, Eerdmans. The *other* standard work, arranged analytically; provides less comprehensive word definitions, but is faster to use. 1

Greek-English Concordances

The Englishman's Greek Concordance of the New Testament, Zondervan. Lists every Greek word in the New Testament according to Greek alphabet and form, passages in which these words occur, and English translations listed according to the King James Version. 2

Greek-English Concordance, J.B. Smith, Herald Press. A tabular and statistical concordance based on the King James Version which enables the reader to see at a glance all the different renderings of any Greek word along with the number of occurrences. Also contains an English-to-Greek index. 2

The New Englishman's Greek Concordance, George V. Wigram, Associated Publishers and Authors. The same work as the *Englishman's Greek Concordance* but keyed to the numbers in *Strong's Concordance.* 1 for those with *Strong's;* otherwise 2

The Word Study New Testament, Ralph D. Winter, ed., William Carey Press, Tyndale, two vols. The King James New Testament in volume one is keyed to Wigram's *Englishman's Greek Concordance* in volume two; the latter is keyed to Arndt and Gingrich's *Greek Lexicon* and Kittel's *Theological Dictionary.* A great timesaver for the non-Greek reader. 1

Greek Concordances

Concordance to the Greek New Testament, Moulton and Geden, Kregel, T. & T. Clark (Edinburgh). The scholar's concordance, useful only to those with an ability to read Greek easily. 3

Handkonkordanz zum Griechischen Neuen Testament, A. Schmöler, W.B.S. (Stuttgart; available from American Bible Society) Like the above, useful only to advanced students. Printed in Germany, but Greek is Greek in any language. 3

Translations

With translations, there are too many (and most are familiar to most readers) to describe individually. All are helpful and all are usable by the beginner.

In regard to standard, modern, and paraphrased translations there may be some difference of opinion as to what constitutes a "standard" version and what does not. The difference in some cases is slight. The list is meant to be helpful, not controversial, and the reader might well choose a work in the modern and paraphrased group as his standard version.

Standard

American Standard Version, 1901
Geneva Bible, 1560 Facsimile edition, University of Wisconsin
King James Version
King James II Version, Jay Green, MacDonald, Associated Publishers and Authors
New American Standard Version
New International Version, Zondervan
Revised Standard Version

Study

Amplified Bible, Zondervan
Emphasized Bible, Joseph Rotheram, Kregel

Interlinear Translations: see Section IX: Greek Testaments

The New Testament: An Expanded Translation, Kenneth Wuest,
Eerdmans
The New Testament from Twenty-Six Translations, Curtis Vaughan,
ed., Zondervan
Young's Literal Translation of the Bible, Robert Young, Baker,
Guardian Press

Modern and Paraphrased

The Bible: A New Translation, James Moffatt, Harper and Row
The Complete Bible: An American Translation, J.M. Powis Smith
and Edgar Goodspeed, University of Chicago
The Epistles of Paul, W.J. Coneybeare, Baker
The Good News Bible: Today's English Version, American Bible
Society
Holy Bible: An American Translation, William Beck, Leader
Holy Bible: The New Berkeley Version in Modern English, Zonder-
van
The Jerusalem Bible, Doubleday
The Living Bible, Paraphrased, Kenneth Taylor, Tyndale
Macknight on the Epistles, James Macknight, Baker
The New English Bible, Oxford and Cambridge
The New Testament in the Language of the People, Charles Wil-
liams, Moody Press
The New Testament in Modern English, J.B. Phillips, Macmillan
The New Testament in Modern Speech, Richard Weymouth, Harper
and Row
The New Testament: A New Translation, William Barclay, Foun-
tain Books

A New Translation of the Holy Bible, J.N. Darby, Kingston Bible Trust (Lancing, England)

Study Bibles

The Companion Bible, Zondervan. KJV text with generous notes relating to words and grammar; emended translations, synonyms distinguished, etc.; 198 appendices supply a wealth of information, much of which is related to language studies. Mostly the work of Dr. E.W. Bullinger. 1

The Harper Study Bible, Harold Lindsell, ed., Zondervan. Text of RSV with helpful notes, introductions, etc.; however, very little relates to original languages. 1

The Newberry Reference Bible, Thomas Newberry, Kregel. A reprint of a late nineteenth-century work. A system of symbols illuminates various features of the grammar of the original. Synonyms, added and deleted words, corrected translations, and (in the New Testament) notes on textual criticism are supplied. Uses the KJV text arranged in paragraph form. 1

The Open Bible, Nelson. KJV text with helpful features but of little help to the language student. 1

The Oxford Annotated Bible, Oxford. RSV text with footnotes and other features, but again only indirectly helpful to the student of Greek. 1

The Ryrie Study Bible, Charles C. Ryrie, Moody. A new work in the Scofield tradition. Provides helpful footnotes and detailed outlines, but very little in regard to word studies or grammar. Available in KJV or NASB text. 1

The Scofield (and *New Scofield*) *Reference Bible,* C.I. Scofield and various editors, Oxford. A classic study Bible (also available in an updated version). Provides considerable information on words and grammar of the originals via footnotes, marginal notes, and suggested word changes. 1

English Word Studies

One-Volume Word Studies

In regard to both English and Greek word studies and commentaries, there are far too many works to list here which consider Greek words and grammar in some respect. Even many layman's commentaries and much Sunday school literature consider the Greek originals to some extent. Here, however, we list only those works *directly* connected with the Greek text and its relation to the English reader.

Expository Dictionary of New Testament Words, W.E. Vine, Revell, MacDonald. A standard tool listing almost every English word in the KJV New Testament, with brief but comprehensive discussions of the Greek word or words from which each is rendered. 1

Light from the Greek New Testament, Boyce W. Blackwelder, Baker Book House A simple introduction to the Greek New Testament, with interesting studies in both vocabulary and grammar. Some interpretations are provocative. 1

New Testament Words, William Barclay, Westminster. Very informative and interesting discussion of a number of important New Testament words. Arranged according to the Greek rather than the English form. 1

Multivolume Word Studies and Commentaries

AMG Series, Spiros Zodhiates, AMG Press. A series of simple studies on the Greek text of various New Testament books, chapters, and passages intended for devotional reading. Includes *A Richer Life for You in Christ* (1 Corinthians 1); *A Revolutionary Mystery* (1 Corinthians 2); *Behaviour of Belief* (James); etc. Very simple and well-suited for the beginner. 1

New Testament Word Studies, J.A. Bengel, two vols., Kregel. A classic work from the eighteenth century. One of the first to consider the importance of approaching the New Testament from a philological standpoint, and a model for many succeeding works. Still an interesting and helpful work. 2

Translator's Handbook Series, various authors, available from American Bible Society. A series of studies on various New Testament books (including Mark, Luke, Acts, Romans, 1 and 2 Thessalonians, 1, 2, and 3 John) that is intended especially for missionary translators. The comments relating to the exegesis of the Greek text are quite simple and suitable for the average Bible student. 2

Word Pictures in the New Testament, A.T. Robertson, six vols., Broadman. A brief but comprehensive discussion of the New Testament book by book. One of the most popular sets, giving word meanings, roots, history, and grammatical insights. 2

Word Studies in the Greek New Testament for the English Reader, Kenneth Wuest, three vols. (also available in sixteen paperback vols.), Eerdmans. The simplest of the word-study sets. Contains both topical and book studies along with an expanded translation of certain books. 1

Word Studies in the New Testament, Marvin R. Vincent, four vols. (Eerdmans edition) or two vols. (MacDonald edition). Book-by-book treatment of the New Testament, with incisive comments, revisions of the text where needed, word histories, etc. 2

Lexicons

Analytical Greek Lexicon to the New Testament, Contains every form of every Greek word in the New Testament (not just the dictionary form of the word), along with a grammatical analysis. Also contains brief word definitions. An essential tool for the English reader who wishes to work directly from the Greek text. 2

Biblico-Theological Lexicon of New Testament Greek, Hermann Cremer, Attic Press. Detailed articles on the theological importance of all the doctrinally important words of the New Testament. 3

A Concise Greek-English Dictionary of the New Testament, B.M. Newman, Jr., American Bible Society. A brief, simple lexicon of the Greek words in the Greek New Testament without extensive definitions or bibliographic data. Excellent for the beginning Greek student. 2

Greek-English Lexicon of the New Testament, W.F. Arndt and F.W. Gingrich, Zondervan. This work (a translation from the German of W. Bauer) is the standard work in its field. Definitions are concise, yet complete. Each entry contains a wealth of bibliographic data. An incredible amount of research went into this tool, which every Greek student should possess and use. A new edition of this work, edited by Gingrich and Danker, is now available. 2

Greek-English Lexicon to the New Testament, Green, Zondervan. A small, inexpensive volume giving concise definitions of the Greek words in the New Testament. 2

Greek-English Lexicon, Liddell and Scott, Oxford. The standard work in the field of classical Greek. It is useful to the student of New Testament Greek for purposes of comparison, word history, etc. 3

Greek-English Lexicon of the New Testament, Joseph Thayer, Zondervan. The standard work of the previous generation. This work is still quite valuable for Thayer's comments and discussions of synonyms, word distinctions, etc. 2

Index to the Arndt-Gingrich Lexicon, John Alsop, Zondervan. A handy tool for the English reader or beginning Greek student; this index opens up this great lexicon to the reader unable easily to locate Greek words in a lexicon. 1

Manual Greek Lexicon of the New Testament, Abbott-Smith, Attic Press. This older work does not make use of more-recent findings in the field of New Testament Greek but is still valuable for the writer's comments. 2

New Testament Word Lists, Morrison and Barnes, Eerdmans. This is not technically a lexicon but is intended as a reading aid for beginning Greek students. It is arranged according to the books of the New Testament, with all the Greek words occurring in a particular chapter (except for words of frequent occurrence, which are listed in a separate appendix) arranged alphabetically with simple definitions. 2

New Thayer's Greek-English Lexicon, Joseph Thayer, Associated Publishers and Authors. The same as Thayer's *Lexicon,* but keyed to the numbers in *Strong's Concordance.* 1 for those with *Strong's*; otherwise 2

Reader's Greek-English Lexicon of the New Testament, Sakae Kubo, Zondervan. Also for the reader of New Testament Greek. This work is listed according to books, chapters, and verses of the New Testament, with words of less-frequent occurrence in a particular verse given simple definitions. Several helpful appendices are included. 2

Shorter Lexicon of the Greek New Testament, F. W. Gingrich, Zondervan. The definitions given in the Arndt-Gingrich *Lexicon* but without the extensive bibliographic data. 2

Vocabulary of the Greek New Testament, Moulton and Milligan, Eerdmans. An essential tool for the serious student. Arranged in lexicon form, this work gives illustrations of the actual usage of New Testament words in ordinary business and domestic documents of early Christian times. 3

Greek Word Studies

One-Volume Word Studies

Synonyms of the New Testament, R.C. Trench, Eerdmans. The standard work on synonyms for several generations. Examines words used synonymously in the New Testament to determine the degree of similarity (or dissimilarity) in meaning between these words. 3

A Treasury of New Testament Synonyms, Steward Custer, Baker. This new study utilizes fresh material to examine the synonymous nature of various New Testament words. 2

Multivolume Word Studies and Commentaries

Alford's Greek Testament, Henry Alford, four vols, in six bindings, Baker Book House. An older work which is still valuable. Contains information on textual criticism, word studies, grammatical insight. Arranged as a verse-by-verse commentary on the New Testament Greek text. 3

Expositor's Greek New Testament, W. Robertson Nicoll, ed., five vols., Eerdmans Exegesis and exposition of the New Testament by great English scholars of a former generation. Very helpful but often technical. 3

New International Dictionary of New Testament Theology, Colin Brown, ed., Zondervan. This three-volume work looks at the important English words in the New Testament from both a philological and a theological standpoint. 2

Theological Dictionary of the New Testament, Kittel and Friedrich, eds., ten vols., Eerdmans. Probably the standard work in its field. This in-depth treatment of theologically important Greek words is definitely not conservative in its approach, but the discriminating Bible student can find much technical help. 3

Grammars

Beginner's Grammar of the Greek New Testament, W.H. Davis, Harper and Row. A simple, concise, but comprehensive treatment of the basics of Greek grammar in the New Testament. The standard work for beginning Greek students in many schools for years. 1

Beginner's Reader-Grammar for New Testament Greek, Colwell and Tune, Harper and Row. More simplified in its approach than the previous work. Teaches the elementary fundamentals and provides a good introduction to more-detailed works. 1

Concise Exegetical Grammar of New Testament Greek, J. Harold Greenlee, Eerdmans. Very brief and concise handbook of important grammatical information needed by the exegete. Helpful for reference purposes for the not-too-advanced student. 1

Elements of New Testament Greek, J.W. Wenham, Cambridge University Press. A textbook with exercises for students (key to exercises available separately). 1

Essentials of New Testament Greek, Ray Summers, Broadman. Like the above, a textbook designed for first-year college students of New Testament Greek. 1

Grammar of New Testament Greek, Moulton-Howard-Turner, 3 vols., Allenson. A classic work (being a revision of a revision dating back several generations), updated and essential as a reference tool for the serious student. 2

Grammar of the Greek New Testament (in the Light of Historical Research), A.T. Robertson, Broadman Press. A mammoth volume which contains a comprehensive treatment of all phases of New Testament Greek grammar. A standard work since its publication in 1914. Robertson's studies in this field are also available in a *Short Grammar* for less-demanding students. 2

Greek Grammar of the New Testament and Other Early Christian Literature, F. Blass and A. DeBrunner, University of Chicago. This great work (translated from the German by Robert Funk) is a modern classic utilizing all the latest discoveries to provide one of the most up-to-date grammars available. 3

Greek Programmed Primer, J.R. Werner, Presbyterian and Reformed. Designed as a three-volume set, the volumes are also available individually. A true primer, it begins with basics and leads the student logically into more-advanced fields of study. 1

Handbook of New Testament Greek: An Inductive Approach Based on the Greek Text of Acts, W.S. LaSor, Eerdmans. This two-volume set contains a vast amount of information but is designed for the beginning student. A first-year course in New Testament Greek based on an inductive study of Acts. 1

Idiom-Book of New Testament Greek, C.F.D. Moule, Cambridge University Press. A more-specialized study of the idiomatic usages of Greek words, phrases, and grammar by various New Testament writers. 3

Language of the New Testament, E.V. Goetchius, Scribners. A workbook to be used in connection with this standard course textbook is also available. 1

Let's Study Greek, Clarence B. Hale, Moody. An inductive method course for first-year Greek students. Teaches the basics of grammar in a simple fashion. 1

Manual Grammar of the Greek New Testament: with Index, Dana and Mantey, Macmillan. A comprehensive but simple-to-understand treatment of the fundamentals of grammar. Useful either as a course book or as a reference tool. The writing style is lucid and interesting. 2

New Testament Greek: An Introductory Grammar, E. Jay, Allenson. A simple introduction to the field of grammatical studies for the beginner. A key to the exercises is also available separately. 1

New Testament Greek For Beginners, J. Gresham Machen, Macmillan. A first-year course used in many seminaries and Bible colleges. Cassettes to be used in conjunction with this work are also available (see section on Study and Correspondence Courses and Tapes). 1

New Testament Greek Notebook, Benjamin Chapman, Baker Book House. Designed for the beginning student. Clear and concise. 1

New Testament Greek Primer, Alfred Marshall, Zondervan. One
of the simpler approaches available. By the author of
an excellent interlinear translation. 1

New Testament Greek: A Workbook For Beginners, S. Hallack, Hallack Publishers. Covers the essentials in workbook format. 1

Syntax of The Moods and Tenses in New Testament Greek, Ernest
Burton, Kregel. Reprint of a classic work. Burton con-
centrates on a specific aspect of Greek grammar—the
verb. An essential reference tool for the serious student. 2

Grammatical Aids

Analytical Greek New Testament, Barbara Friberg and Timothy
Friberg, eds., Baker. The complete text of the Greek
New Testament with interlinear "tags" or abbrevia-
tions which analyze the text grammatically. 2

Card-Guide to the Greek New Testament, Benjamin Chapman,
Baker. A laminated, notebook-size card containing essential information on the Greek alphabet, noun declensions, verb paradigms, etc. Designed as a handy
reference tool for the busy Greek student. 2

Grammatical Aids for Students of New Testament Greek, Walter
Mueller, Eerdmans. Charts, verb paradigms, and other
essential information for the Greek student. Designed
to be used with a standard grammar, not as a course
in itself. 2

Grammatical Analysis of the Greek New Testament, Max Zerwick,
Two vols, Biblical Institute Press (Rome). Verse-
by-verse analysis with information on both meanings
and grammatical force of important words. 2

Grammatical Insights into the New Testament, Nigel Turner, Allenson. Neither a grammar nor exactly a word-study volume, this work considers various New Testament
passages from a grammatical viewpoint and is fascinat-

ing reading for the student with some knowledge of New Testament Greek, may be somewhat difficult for the non-Greek reader. 2

Greek Slide-a-Verb Chart, David Peterson, Zondervan. A handy slide-rule-type tool designed to show quickly the various inflections of the Greek verb. 2

Lexical Aids for Students of New Testament Greek, Bruce Metzger, Allenson. Vocabulary lists and other helpful information (including a valuable and often-reprinted preposition chart) intended for use by the student in connection with his standard tools. 2

Linguistic Key to the Greek New Testament, Fritz Rienecker, two vols., Zondervan. Important words in each verse analyzed as to meaning and grammatical import. Helpful as a reference tool for the beginning Greek student or English reader. 2

Manual of Greek Forms, James Boyer, BMH Books. Various charts of noun declensions, verb paradigms, and other essential information arranged in a handy format for the busy student. 2

Parsing Guide to the Greek New Testament, Nathan Han, Herald Press. Arranged verse-by-verse. Every verb in the Greek Testament analyzed, with dictionary form indicated. Must be used in conjunction with a Greek Testament and a standard lexicon. 2

Greek Testaments

The Greek New Testament, Aland, Black, Martini, Metzger, Wikgren, eds., American Bible Society. The product of many hours of research, this work belongs in the library of every serious Bible student. Contains English subheadings and ample critical notes for the exegete, expositor, or missionary translator. 2

Hē Kainē Diathēkē, Textus Receptus; various editions of the Received Text are available from the American Bible

Society, Trinitarian Bible Society, and other publishers. 2

Interlinear Greek-English New Testaments; the student's choice among the various ones available will probably depend upon his preference in Greek texts; Alfred Marshall's translation (based on the Nestle text) is available in several editions from Zondervan; George Berry's interlinear (based on the Received Text) is available from Baker, Zondervan, Broadman, MacDonald, and others; Jay Green's version (based on the form of the Greek text found in the KJV) is available both separately and as a part of the *Interlinear Bible* (containing both Hebrew and Greek texts with interlinear and marginal translations) from Associated Publishers and Authors; all are helpful. 1

Novum Testamentum Graece, Nestle, et al, eds., available from the American Bible Society; the scholar's Greek Testament and the basis for many modern translations; contains gospel parallels, references, and a wealth of critical data. 2

Works on Textual Criticism

Encountering New Testament Manuscripts, Jack Finegan, Eerdmans. A textbook offering students an exciting approach to the field of textual criticism by encountering the original manuscripts themselves (by means of reproductions). 2

Introduction to New Testament Textual Criticism, J. Harold Greenlee, Eerdmans. A textbook introducing this vast field in a comprehensive manner, yet simple to understand. 2

Text of the New Testament: Its Transmission, Corruption and Restoration, Bruce M. Metzger, Oxford. Perhaps the standard textbook in this field by an acknowledged master of the subject. 3

Textual Commentary on the Greek New Testament, Bruce M. Metzger, American Bible Society. The companion to the
ABS Greek New Testament. Explores the methods and
reasoning behind the critical choices made in forming
that text. 3

Study and Correspondence Courses and Tapes

Learn or Review New Testament Greek, AMG press. The vocabularies and exercises from J. Gresham Machen's *New
Testament Greek for Beginners* (see Grammar section)
recorded on nine cassettes by Spiros Zodhiates. Helpful for Greek students or those having trouble with
pronunciation of Greek words. 2

New Testament Greek Correspondence Course, Moody Bible Institute Correspondence School. Available in two parts,
each part equivalent to one semester of college Greek.
Contains textbook, cassettes (or open-reel tapes), Greek
Testament, lexicon. Each part earns four college cred-
its. 1

Do It Yourself Hebrew and Greek, Edward Goodrick, Zondervan/
Multnomah. An introduction to both languages (much
more space is allotted to Greek than to Hebrew), with
basic fundamentals covered and tear-out lesson sheets
in the back. Also contains a cassette for the student
who wishes to learn how to pronounce both languages
correctly. 1

Miscellaneous Works

The Minister and His Greek New Testament, A.T. Robertson, Baker
Book House. Various essays by the great Greek scholar
on the importance of the Greek Testament to the minister or Christian worker, as well as interesting studies
in vocabulary, grammar, and the papyri. 2

Synopsis Quattuor Evangeliorum, Kurt Aland, American Bible Society. This work (also available in a Greek-English ver-

sion but with some material deleted) is a synopsis of the four Gospels in Greek with parallels from apocryphal gospels and patristic sources. Helpful tool for scholars and Greek readers. 3

The Septuagint—Selected Aids

Concordance of the Septuagint, George Morrish, Zondervan. A handy tool (and essential for the student of the LXX) which lists only the verses where a particular word occurs, rather than printing out the passage in full. Easily usable, however, by the student with some knowledge of Greek. 2

The Septuagint, A. Rahlfs, ed., available from the American Bible Society. This work (a German product available in two volumes) is a scholarly and critical edition of the LXX. An essential tool for the serious student of the LXX. 3

The Septuagint: Greek and English, Zondervan (available both with and without the Apocrypha). This work contains an English translation by Sir Launcelot Lee Brenton in the margin along with the complete Greek text and is thus much easier for the English reader to use. 1 for English translation, 2 for Greek text

The Hebrew Bible—Selected Aids

Scriptures

Biblia Hebraica, R. Kittel, ed., available from the American Bible Society. The scholar's text of the Hebrew Old Testament and the basis for most modern versions. Contains ample critical data. 3

Englishman's Linear Hebrew-English Old Testament (Genesis to 2 Samuel), J. Magil, ed., Zondervan. Hebrew text with a literal English text printed by the side (not underneath). 1 for English translation, 3 for Hebrew text

Hebrew-English Old Testament, Zondervan. From the Bagster
Polyglot Series. Contains the Massoretic text of the
Hebrew with the Authorized Version alongside. 1 for
the English, 3 for the Hebrew

Hebrew Scriptures, various editions published by the British and
Foreign Bible Society, Hebrew Publishing Co., and others, available from the American Bible Society; budget
editions of the Massoretic text. 3

Concordances

Englishman's Hebrew and Chaldee Concordance of the Old Testament,
Zondervan. Every major word in the Hebrew Bible
arranged in Hebrew form according to the Hebrew
alphabet, with the passages where each word occurs
listed underneath in the KJV. 2

New Englishman's Hebrew and Chaldee Concordance, Associated
Publishers and Authors. The same work as above, but
keyed to the numbers in *Strong's Concordance.* 1 for
those with *Strong's,* otherwise 2

Lexicons

Analytical Hebrew and Chaldee Lexicon, Zondervan, MacDonald.
Every word in the Hebrew Bible analyzed grammatically, with dictionary form listed. Brief definitions are
also given. An essential tool for the English reader. 2

Hebrew and Chaldee Lexicon, Tregelles Translation, William Gesenius, Eerdmans. A classic lexicon still much in use.
Comprehensive and scholarly. 2

Hebrew-English Lexicon, Zondervan. A simple lexicon for the
beginning student. Definitions are very brief. 2

Hebrew-English Lexicon, Brown, Driver, and Briggs, Oxford. A
great standard work, but somewhat difficult for the
student to use due to the placement of entries according to triconsonantal roots rather than regular alphabetical form. Indexes are available, however. 3

Lexicon in Veteris Testamenti Libros: Hebrew Aramaic Lexicon, Koehler and Baumgartner, Eerdmans. Entries given in both German and English. The most up-to-date tool available. Essential for the scholar. 2

Word Studies

Commentary on the Old Testament, Keil and Delitzsch, ten vols. The standard commentary on the Hebrew text for generations. Scholarly and comprehensive, but requires reading ability in Hebrew. 3

Dictionary of Old Testament Words for English Readers, Aaron Pick, Kregel. The Old Testament equivalent of *Vine's New Testament Dictionary*; listed according to English words, with brief discussions of the Hebrew word or words underlying each. 1

Synonyms of the Old Testament, Robert Girdlestone, Eerdmans. The Old Testament equivalent of Trench's *Synonyms.* Almost as concerned with the LXX and the New Testament as with the Hebrew. Fascinating reading, but not nearly as detailed as Trench's work. 2

Grammars

Gesenius Hebrew Grammar, William Gesenius, Oxford University Press. The standard and most comprehensive reference tool. Covers the entire field of Hebrew grammar. 3

Beginner's Handbook to Biblical Hebrew, John Marks and Virgil Rogers, Abingdon. A workbook for this introductory first-year textbook is also available. Good for the beginner. 1

Introductory Hebrew Grammar, Laird Harris, Eerdmans. Very simple and concise. Contains exercises. 1

Miscellaneous Works

Hebrew Language Chart, J. J. Davis, Baker. A laminated chart with information and paradigm for the Hebrew strong verb. Handy reference tool for the busy student. 2

Hebrew Slide-a-Verb Chart, Peterson and Barker, Zondervan. A slide-rule-type chart showing quickly and easily the various grammatical changes which the Hebrew verb can undergo. 2

Hebrew Vocabularies, J. Barton Payne, Baker. For the beginning Hebrew student wishing to increase his vocabulary. Nouns and verbs are listed according to frequency of occurrence in the Hebrew Bible. 2

Index to Brown-Driver-Briggs Lexicon, Bruce Einspahr, Moody. A handy tool arranged verse-by-verse with the help of a computer. This work makes this great lexicon easily usable by the beginning student. 2

ACKNOWLEDGMENTS

The following publishers and individuals have kindly granted permission to quote from their works:

Abingdon Press, Nashville, Tennessee
  Strong's Exhaustive Concordance, J. Strong
Associated Publishers and Authors, Lafayette, Indiana
  New Englishman's Hebrew Concordance
  The Interlinear Greek-English New Testament
Back To The Bible Broadcast, Lincoln, Nebraska
  Witnessing to the Cults, H. J. Berry
  Good News Broadcaster, ed., T. H. Epp
Baker Book House, Grand Rapids, Michigan
  Expository Preaching for Today, A. W. Blackwood
  A Card Guide to the New Testament, A. W. Blackwood
  A Card Guide to the New Testament Exegesis, B. Chapman
Walter De Gruyter and Company, Berlin, West Germany
  *A Greek-English Lexicon to the Greek New Testament and
    Other Early Christian Literature,* W. F. Arndt and F. W.
    Gingrich
William B. Eerdmans Publishing Company, Grand Rapids,
    Michigan
  Concise Exegetical Grammar of the New Testament, J. H.
    Greenlee
  Handbook of the New Testament Greek, W. S. LaSor
  Vocabulary of the Greek New Testament, J. H. Moulton and
    G. Milligan
  Expositor's Greek Testament, W. R. Nicoll
  Synonyms of the New Testament, R. C. Trench
  Word Studies in the New Testament, M. R. Vincent

Untranslatable Riches From the Greek Testament, K. Wuest

Philippians in the Greek New Testament, K. Wuest

Studies in the Vocabulary of the Greek New Testament: An Expanded Translation, K. Wuest

Young's Analytical Concordance to the Bible, R. Young

Harper and Row Publishers, Inc., New York, New York

The Bible: A New Translation, J. B. Moffatt

Beginner's Reader-Grammar for New Testament Greek, Colwell and Tune

God's Word in Man's Language, E. Nida

Ancestry of our English Bible, Price

Herald Press, Scottdale, Pennsylvania

Parsing Guide to the Greek New Testament, N. Han

Kregel Publications, Grand Rapids, Michigan

Syntax of Moods and Tenses in New Testament Greek, E. Burton

Newberry Reference Bible, T. Newberry

The Lockman Foundation, La Habra, California

New American Standard Bible

Loyola University Press, Chicago, Illinois

Grammatical Analysis of Greek New Testament, M. Zerwick

Macmillan Publishing Company, Inc., New York, New York

The New Testament in Modern English, J. B. Phillips

A Manual Grammar of New Testament Greek, H. E. Dana and J. E. Mantey

Moody Press, Chicago, Illinois

The New Testament in the Language of the People, C. B. Williams

Frank N. Potter

Is That in the Bible?, C. F. Potter

Bruce M. Metzger

Lexical Aids for Students of New Testament Greek, B. Metzger

Fleming H. Revell Company, Old Tappan, New Jersey

Expository Dictionary of New Testament Words, W. E. Vine

Oxford University Press, New York, New York
  The New Scofield Reference Bible, C. I. Scofield
  Semantices of Biblical Language, J. Barr
Charles Scribner's Sons, New York, New York
  The Epistles of Paul, W. J. Coneybeare
  Romans, Sanday and Headlam
The Sunday School Board of the Southern Baptist
        Convention, Nashville, Tennessee
  Word Pictures in the New Testament, A. T. Robertson
The University of Chicago Press, Chicago, Illinois
  The Complete Bible: An American Translation, Smith, Powis,
        and Goodspeed
The Westminster Press, Philadelphia, Pennsylvania
  The New Testament: A New Translation, W. Barclay
  New Testament Words, W. Barclay
The Zondervan Corporation, Grand Rapids, Michigan
  *The Modern Language Bible: The Berkeley Version in Modern
        English*
  The Companion Bible, E. W. Bullinger
  The Interlinear Greek-English New Testament, A. Marshall